0 1341 1154427 3

2009 01 19

D1606526

Macrosociology

DATE DUE	RETURNED
NOV 2 4 2009	NOV 2 6 2009

Macrosociology
Four Modern Theorists

Frank W. Elwell

165101

Paradigm Publishers
Boulder • London

Copyright © 2006 Paradigm Publishers

Published in the United States by Paradigm Publishers, 3360 Mitchell Lane Suite E, Boulder, CO 80301 USA.

Paradigm Publishers is the trade name of Birkenkamp & Company, LLC, Dean Birkenkamp, President and Publisher.

Library of Congress Cataloging-in-Publication Data
Elwell, Frank W.
  Macrosociology : four modern theorists / Frank W. Elwell.
    p. cm.
  Includes bibliographical references and index.
  ISBN: 978-1-59451-257-5 (hc)   ISBN: 978-1-59451-258-2 (pbk.)
  1. Macrosociology. 2. Mills, C. Wright (Charles Wright), 1916–
1962. 3. Harris, Marvin, 1927– 4. Wallerstein, Immanuel Maurice,
1930– 5. Lenski, Gerhard Emmanuel, 1924–   I. Title.
  HM490.E48 2006
  301.092'2—dc22

                                                          2006001595

Printed and bound in the United States of America on acid free paper that meets the standards of the American National Standard for Permanence of Paper for Printed Library Materials.

10 09 08 07   2 3 4 5

For C. Duke Wilder

But if we proceed without a thorough knowledge and accurate comprehension of the nature, extent, and magnitude of the difficulties we have to encounter, or if we unwisely direct our efforts towards an object in which we cannot hope for success, we shall not only exhaust our strength in fruitless exertions and remain at as great a distance as ever from the summit of our wishes, but we shall be perpetually crushed by the recoil of this rock of Sisyphus.

—T. Robert Malthus, 1798

Contents

Acknowledgments

I wish to acknowledge that I have been strongly influenced by my family and friends. I have also been powerfully affected by the society in which I was born as well as the one it has become. I believe I have also been molded by my role as son, brother, father, student, bus boy, factory worker, ice cream man, teacher, professor, and dean, as well as the other roles I have taken throughout my life. In addition, there have been myths that have permeated my consciousness, ideologies to which I have been exposed—some even believed. Finally, I owe much to books and articles that I have read, music I have listened to, TV and movies that I have watched, and acquaintances and strangers who have had some affect on my perceptions and opinion. While this has been true in life, it is also true in the writing of this book. I thank all who had a hand in it. I take full responsibility for all.

Prologue: The Past

Mainstream sociology is straying from its roots. This can be clearly seen in introductory sociology and social problems texts in which a focus on microsociology and social psychology has become ever more prominent. It can also be seen in the more recent graduates of sociology programs, specialists in one or two of the more than thirty subfields of sociology. While all tend to be well versed in questionnaire design and data manipulation as well as being excellent specialists in such diverse fields as gerontology or deviance, most have little background in the broader traditions of the discipline, little appreciation or experience with holistic analyses.

Today, too many sociologists practice the discipline as one of social data collection and manipulation, a reification of method over substance. Others are specializing in a small part of the sociocultural system—say family, or deviance, or criminality—and losing the inclination or ability to communicate with their colleagues and their students either in other subfields or about the larger social whole. Some still do continue the practice of macrosociology, but it too is often the preserve of specialists with their own jargon, interests, and readership.

While theory is still required in most of the undergraduate and graduate level programs, theory is too often taught as history. Robert K. Merton was fond of quoting Alfred North Whitehead that "a science which hesitates to forget its founders is lost." He argues that social scientists today must move beyond the founders in constructing social theory. However, he does not advocate that we need to reinvent our theoretical perspectives from whole cloth. Rather, we must be selective in our use of the substance of certain theories that have proved their usefulness and utility in explaining/predicting sociocultural phenomena, and jettison the rest. He maintains that many sociologists have confused the history of social theory with the systematic development of theory. And this, he says, is both artless and hurtful for the development of social theory itself (1968, pp. 1–38). It is this merging of theory and history that makes theory marginal in the social sciences today. Mastering theory as history, our students lose sight of the relevant substance, isolating theory from the rest of the discipline.

This book intends to go back to the roots of the discipline, back to the macro theories of Malthus, Marx, Weber, and Durkheim. What interests me in these classical writers is their ability to help us understand what is going on in the sociocultural world today. These men, writing in essentially agrarian societies undergoing the initial thrust of the industrial revolution, forecast a future industrial society with such a high degree of accuracy that many have interpreted their work as description rather than prediction (Kumar, 1978). But rather than yet another book that summarizes their theoretical worldview and insights, this work will take a different route.[1] I am not interested in presenting their ideas as historical artifacts. I intend to select the ideas that have special relevance for understanding the contemporary social world. I intend to discipline these insights with the years of criticism, empirical data, and experience that have occurred since their writings. To do this, I will focus on four contemporary practitioners of macrosociology who have borrowed heavily from this tradition, extended it where necessary, and applied it successfully in explaining the sociocultural world. By focusing on four recent practitioners I hope to interest a new generation of sociology students in the excitement and rewards of holistic analyses.

II

The central task of this prologue is to introduce and explain the selection of social theorists who are given primary coverage in this book. I used several criteria for selection. The first, of course, was that the theorist had to focus on the macrolevel, that is, had to analyze social phenomena and human behavior in terms of entire sociocultural systems. This, I believe, characterized the classical theories of Malthus, Marx, Weber, and Durkheim and was one of the reasons that attracted me to the discipline—the promise of understanding human social behavior.

A second criteria used in selecting theorists is that they had to exhibit a healthy respect for the classical tradition. The theorists selected have each been profoundly influenced by parts of this tradition. C. Wright Mills, for example, co-authored a major work on Max Weber,[2] and wrote throughout his life on the importance and usefulness of the classical tradition in understanding the human condition. In *The*

Sociological Imagination, for example, Mills writes of the importance of classic analysis. "I believe that what may be called classic social analysis is a definable and usable set of traditions; that its essential feature is the concern with historical social structures; and that its problems are of direct relevance to urgent public issues and insistent human troubles" (1959, p. 21). I believe these public issues are even more urgent today, human troubles even more insistent. I also believe that parts of the classical tradition are still of great relevance.

The predominant classical influence on the macro-analyses of C. Wright Mills is clearly Max Weber. Mills's analyses of contemporary American society give strong emphasis to the growth in the size and reach of bureaucratic organizations. His work can easily be interpreted as an elaboration of the consequences of this growth on American character and institutional structures. And it is an analysis that still resonates today.

Marvin Harris might be considered by some to be a somewhat quirky choice for inclusion in this volume. Although Harris's theory of cultural materialism is a prime example of a comprehensive macro-theory of sociocultural systems, he is an anthropologist. If sociologists know the perspective of cultural materialism at all it is often knowledge of a more simplistic version of the strategy that is summarized and then torn apart by critics. The fact that Harris's cultural materialism is so little known within sociology is surprising in some respects. Although coming from a different discipline, the perspective shares several themes with sociology such as functionalism, a concern with demography, and positivism to name a few. While the major classical influences on Harris are Malthus and Marx, he is also well versed in much of the same theoretical tradition as sociologists. Durkheim, Weber, and Spencer and a host of others in the sociological canon are dealt with in Harris's *The Rise of Anthropological Theory* (1968), a seminal work in Cultural Anthropology.[3] Like sociology (perhaps more so than cultural anthropology), Harris's perspective is firmly based in science and empiricism. Still, the perspective is rarely mentioned in sociology texts and scholarship, scarcely given passing mention in our courses.

But given the breadth of sociology and the explosion of books, articles and data about all aspects of social life, it is perhaps understandable that many sociologists are not familiar with cultural materialism. Many can barely keep up with their own more narrow specialization let alone be well versed in the general epistemological and theoretical debates in a related field. Also, as an anthropologist, Harris has primarily been concerned with applying the perspective to the traditional societies of hunters and gatherers, horticulturists, and pastoralists—societal types that are not considered central in the sociological tradition.

Harris, however, claims to have developed a universal analytical strategy, a theoretical strategy of equal relevance to hunting and gathering, horticultural, and even industrial societies. Such a claim, particularly when made by a social scientist of the stature and obvious heft of Marvin Harris,[4] should attract more attention and investigation within sociology (and attract its share of adherents, as it has in anthropology). The chapter on Harris, then, is intended as a comprehensive summary of his research strategy of cultural materialism. On this occasion of the reissue (2001) of his two primary texts detailing the roots and branches of the perspective, *The Rise of Anthropological Theory* and *Cultural Materialism*, the chapter is especially intended to interest sociologists and our students in this comprehensive research strategy.

The third theorist to be covered is Immanuel Wallerstein, the author of world-systems analyses, who has been strongly influenced by Karl Marx.[5] However, he offers quite a twist to traditional Marxist interpretations. He begins with the proposition that to fully understand modern social life we must start from the proper unit of analysis, that is, the entire social system. He defines the total social system as containing the complete division of labor necessary to meet the needs of the vast majority of people within its boundaries. There have only been three types of such systems throughout history. These are the small, self-contained societies of prehistory, the world-empires of ancient times, and the modern economic world-system. The elaboration of the structures and evolution of the capitalist world-system then provides the context for Wallerstein's explanation of modern social life. In his analysis Wallerstein deals successfully with such issues as social class, racism, inequality, ideology, and the actions of nation states. All, he claims, can only be understood in the context of the entire world-system.

The fourth and final theorist covered in this book, Gerhard Lenski, is again a more conventional choice. He is a sociologist; he has long been an advocate for macrolevel theory in the discipline, early in his career seeming to be alone in this endeavor among his contemporaries. Reading Lenski, one can readily see the influence of all who went before. Lenski's goal is to create a macrosocial theory capable of integrating the most powerful explanatory schemes offered in the past. Beginning with Malthus, Lenski has borrowed from a variety of classical theorists; he has also been influenced by Mills, Harris, and Wallerstein as well. Lenski has spent the bulk of his career synthesizing, testing, and refining his ecological-evolutionary theory of sociocultural stability and change. As a result, his macrosociological theory is a comprehensive beginning framework for ordering and understanding the nature and behavior of sociocultural systems.

While the four theorists selected for inclusion in this book have been heavily influenced by traditional macrolevel social theory, they share some other characteristics as well. Each of the four theorists selected is exciting, each of them passing my own personal "aha test"— offering both a unique perspective and significant insight on human social life and behavior. All four, of course, were active in the latter half of the twentieth century; all were reacting to their history and to national and international events around them. All four have a strong commitment to social science as science, insisting that empirical study provide the necessary discipline to theoretical speculation. Each has had influence on thousands of social scientists and students around the globe. Finally, while each was successful in his professional field, they each tried to share their social science with a broader audience as well. They are in agreement that social science can contribute to our understanding of sociocultural systems. They are in agreement that these sociocultural systems have enormous impact on our lives. They each believe that the study of such sociocultural forces gives enormous intrinsic satisfaction—gives coherence, meaning, and understanding to experiences and observations that often seem random, incoherent, or obscure. Further, they believe that understanding these forces can help us in making better decisions in our lives, as individuals and as members of our societies. It is only through understanding sociocultural systems and the impact of these forces on individuals that we can hope to collectively control our fate by our reason.[6]

In writing this book I did not think it my task to heavily critique these theorists. I believe that there is often a conflict of interest between the tasks of exposition and criticism when it comes to dealing with social theory. To shine in the role of critic, authors oftentimes set up straw men, avoiding the subtleties and caveats of the theorist under examination in order to score cheap points or add their own personal twists to the theory.[7] I see my role here as different. As famed historian Leopold von Ranke put it, our job as historians is to present history "wie es eignetlich gewesen ist" (as it actually was). While this goal may be unattainable in most areas of history, it is a realistic goal in intellectual history. My goal, therefore, is to present and document each theory as accurately, as comprehensively, and in as straightforward a manner as possible, "wie es eignetlich gewessen ist."

My intended audience is that of undergraduate social science majors as well as readers with a general interest in the social sciences. The book may also well serve graduate students and established social scientists who wish to venture outside their specialties. Parallel to traditional theory texts in their treatment of classical theorists, the goal of this book is to give the reader a comprehensive introduction to four modern day macrotheorists. While nothing will substitute for actually reading the original works, I know that this is not always possible given the time and specialty constraints of most. And these constraints are a tragedy, for there is no more intrinsically satisfying and fascinating area of study than sociocultural systems and the human condition.

III

When it comes to describing contemporary society it is clear that there is a need to go beyond the categories of political, economic, and technological systems of the past. The old characterizations just do not seem to encompass the new realities around us. "Democracy" calls forth images of limited government, rational discussion and debate of major issues, and choice and compromise at the ballot box. All of this is obviously a far cry from the contemporary political scene with the rise of mass media campaigns, Internet and twenty-four hour news, big money, intense interest group factionalism, and professional campaign managers and manipulators.

"Capitalism" calls forth images of small companies owned by entrepreneurs, competing fiercely for the consumer's dollar in terms of price and quality—again an image somewhat at variance with today's huge corporations, owned by thousands of stockholders, coordinated by interlocking corporate boards, and managed by corporate executives and bureaucrats. Many such corporations rely on government contracts for the bulk of their sales, government overpayment for the bulk of their profits. Many more rely on government regulation (often written by former industry executives), or huge advertising budgets, or new consumption institutions designed to stimulate demand.

"Industrial society" calls forth images of factories, mass production, and assembly lines. Even the big oligopolies of our recent past, with their seeming life-time employment guarantees, stable market shares, choreographed competition, padded bureaucracies, and well-paid workforce seem to be a thing of the past. Now the "global" economy has led to intense competition for American companies. And this has led to downsizing, a consequent rise in contingency work, tightening managerial coordination, capital flight to third world countries or automation, a squeezing of working and middle class wages, and the loss of manufacturing jobs and a rise in service and information jobs.

In response to the seeming disconnect between contemporary society and these old images, some social scientists have come up with a couple of new labels to characterize present day American society. Among sociologists the predominant characterization is that of a "post-industrial society," among anthropologists the image tends to be one of "postmodernism." Postindustrialism posits a new society based on high-tech production that ultimately transforms the entire society. More extreme variants posit this high technology transforming the entire society, demanding a more educated workforce, and ultimately leading to a more just and equitable society. Postmodernists, in contrast, seem to be most unified in their suspicion about empirical social science and hostility toward both traditional and contemporary macrosocial theories. They insist upon the uniqueness of social events, the impossibility of social science ever encompassing the chaos and disorder of the social world in a holistic worldview. Rather, postmodernists advocate understanding events from a multitude of differing interpretations, perspectives that they consider equally valid in describing and interpreting the social world.

The major problem with such "post" characterizations is that they cut off understanding and analyses of contemporary society from history. By positing a society that is "post" industrial or "post" modern, the observer is positing a decisive break of contemporary society from its history and from all previous attempts to understand or describe it. This is foreign to mainstream social science just as it is foreign to human experience itself. While the postmodernists and postindustrialists are correct in asserting that contemporary American society represents something different from the past, they do not make a convincing case that these differences render the past meaningless.

Mills, Harris, Wallerstein, and Lenski are all strongly rooted in the past—each has an unusual command of history and traditional social theory. While their perspectives and emphases differ, each has a worldview of a sociocultural system in which history, ever-intensifying production processes, huge populations, ever-larger bureaucracies, as well as capitalist organizations, are interrelated and have dramatic effect on our environment, our institutions, as well as our personal behavior, beliefs, and values. They each describe a sociocultural system in which community, family, education, politics, medicine, and other institutions are rapidly being redefined, a system in which traditional values and beliefs are constantly re-evaluated and reinterpreted. They each describe a system in which, to quote William Faulkner, "the past isn't dead. It isn't even past."

NOTES

1. For readers who need a quick refresher on any one of the four classical theorists who have had strong influence on the American theorists presented in this book, I have written introductory essays on each off of the following Web page: http://www.faculty.rsu.edu/~felwell/Theorists/Four/index.html. They are on the Web rather than in the opening chapters because I wanted to keep the focus of the main body of this work on contemporary macrotheory rather than yet another history of this theory.

2. *From Max Weber: Essays in Sociology* with Hans Gerth. 1946: Oxford University Press.

3. Trying to draw hard and fast disciplinary boundaries between sociology and anthropology is very difficult. Some assert that the major distinction is in subject matter. Sociologists tend to be concerned with industrial societies, anthropologists with hunting and gathering and horticultural societies (leaving agrarian or agricultural societies to the historians). However, as more and more societies are transitioning to industrialism, more anthropologists are studying industrial societies. Also, in an effort to test the universality of their theories, some anthropologists are applying them to industrial societies (Harris would be a prime example of this). Meanwhile, many sociologists have come to discover the limitations of focusing exclusively on industrial societies and are increasingly examining the anthropological and historical literature to broaden their perspectives (Lenski, the theorist dealt with in Chapter 4, is a prime example of this). So, what is the difference between the two disciplines? One answer is that they have slightly different traditions; slightly different methods, concepts, and theories. But all these differences are relatively minor; practitioners on both sides often cross disciplinary boundaries. Except for the accidents of history and the consequent hold of tradition and self-interest on the practitioners, the two disciplines could easily be merged.

4. Harris published seventeen books and numerous articles, including major texts on anthropological theory, general, and cultural anthropology. Harris was also a past chairman of the General Anthropology Division of the American Anthropological Association.

5. Wallerstein also owes much to Weber for his concepts of formal and substantive rationality.

6. All have also won widespread acclaim in their field but not necessarily as serious social theorists. Such titles usually go to the specialized, those who write arcane, dense prose. Mills was far more notorious as a social critic and gadfly. Harris was seen in anthropology, especially by the postmoderns increasingly dominating his field, as a mere [and misguided] popularizer; he was not

widely known in sociology at all. Wallerstein's theory, unfortunately, often gets lost in a sea of historical detail as well as in his harsh critiques of American foreign policy. And Lenski is [mistakenly] seen by many as a "mere" textbook author—albeit of a hugely successful alternative introductory text. However, each of them has developed sophisticated theories that undergird all of their work.

7. In truth, I have long been struck by the shoddiness of many secondary sources. It seems that once errors of misinterpretation get into this literature they are rarely corrected in subsequent treatments. I was especially appalled with the treatment of Malthus's *1798 Essay* that I found in the literature. Most reviewers had apparently only read misleading secondary sources about the *Essay* rather than the work itself. Or, if they had read the original *Essay*, the secondary literature had so completely biased them against it that they completely mangled his thought. I have also seen critiques of each of the four theorists covered in this volume that seriously misrepresent the theory under discussion.

1

The Sociology of
C. Wright Mills

C. Wright Mills is among a select group of sociologists in the twentieth century who write within the classical tradition. Consistent with the founders of the discipline, Mills attempted interpretive analysis of phenomena within a holistic context of a total sociocultural system. In addition, he has dealt with issues and problems that matter to people, not just to other social scientists. He has written about American society in a way to further the understanding, not only of other sociologists, but of broader publics as well.

In the 1950s Mills wrote about the growth in size and scope of bureaucracies in modern societies from a neoclassical theoretical perspective. Bureaucratic power now confronts citizens everywhere, he claimed, and the resulting concentration of authority affects those who hold it and those who are subject to it. It has dramatic affect on institutions such as family, polity, science, education, and economy. The growth of bureaucracy has also caused the proliferation of white-collar occupations, which profoundly affects the values and perceptions of the people who hold these jobs. Mills also wrote about the ideology and material interests of elites, the rise of militarism and military solutions, and the meaning of communist revolutions and the cold war politics of his day. Most forcefully, he chastised his colleagues about the proper role of social science in exploring and clarifying these and other central issues of the time.

While the secondary literature on Mills often has remarked on the influence of Marx and Veblen on his sociology—and these two theorists certainly have affected his theory—it was Max Weber who had the greater impact. In an application for a Guggenheim grant in 1944, Mills wrote the following about his intellectual influences: "In sociology my main impulse has been taken from German developments, especially the traditions stemming from Max Weber and, to a lesser degree, Karl Mannheim" (Mills, 2000, p. 79). The Guggenheim was granted, and

Mills used it to fund research for his book *White Collar*. In 1957 Mills wrote a letter to the editor of *Commentary* in which he discussed his Marxian influence as well.

> Let me say explicitly: I happen never to have been what is called "a Marxist," but I believe Karl Marx one of the most astute students of society modern civilization has produced; his work is now essential equipment of any adequately trained social scientist as well as of any properly educated person. Those who say they hear Marxian echoes in my work are saying that I have trained myself well. That they do not intend this testifies to their own lack of proper education. (Mills, 2000, p. 237)

Irving Horowitz (1983, pp. 117–147), his biographer, had made much of Mills's early training in American pragmatism, particularly of the influence of John Dewey, William James, and George Herbert Mead. This seems to be particularly true of Mills's social psychology. However, in his macrosociological work Mills was far more influenced by the Europeans. To say that Mills was a Weberian, however, is not to imply that he slavishly followed Weber's every lead.

In all of his work Mills interpreted the world through a coherent theoretical perspective. He used this theory to explain social structures and processes, rather than obscuring them (either intentionally or inadvertently) through data and jargon. Like the classical theory of the discipline, Mills's is a holistic vision of entire sociocultural systems, this system is interdependent, and it has profound effects on human values, thought, and behavior. Consequently, like the classical theorists, his works remain quite relevant and useful today in efforts to understand social reality—to understand what is going on "out there."

Mills was also a very gifted writer. He demonstrated a gift for frank and forthright expression.[1] This was particularly true in his later years when he took to writing social criticism rather than straight academic prose, with little of the cant and caveat of the modern social scientist. *White Collar*, despite some lapses, is Mills at his most sociological. Beginning with *The Power Elite*, published in 1956, Mills became far more polemical and critical in his language.[2]

Even in his writings as a social critic, however, Mills was always consistent with his overall theory of sociocultural systems and his vision of the role of social science within that system. As a social critic, Mills stirred great controversy among his colleagues and among the broader public. Most modern-day treatments of Mills continue to focus on these controversies.

The body of literature that now surrounds Mills is generally distinguished only by its tendency to respond to this outsized reputation and audacious personality, rather than to the ideas they embroidered. To many of his colleagues, he appeared an abrasive and even irresponsible sociologist, his contentious manner hardly worthy of the detached, scientific ideals to which their discipline aspired. (Summers, 2000, p. 4)

To date, few authors have attempted to summarize his theory in a single comprehensive statement. This chapter will focus on the vision that informs his critique, the sociological theory behind C. Wright Mills.

Mills's main body of work centers on the themes of the expansion and centralization of bureaucratic coordination and the consequent "rationalization" of social life. Rationalization is the practical application of knowledge to achieve a desired end. Its goal is efficiency, and its means are total coordination and control over the social processes needed to attain that goal. It is the guiding principle behind bureaucracy and the increasing division of labor. Weber saw it as the hallmark of modern society.

For example, *White Collar* can be viewed as an elaboration and update on Weber's bureaucratization process, detailing the effects of the increasing division of labor on the tone and character of American social life. *The Power Elite* is an exploration of rational-legal bureaucratic authority and its effects on the wielders and subjects of this power. In this work Mills detailed the enlargement and centralization of public and private bureaucracies and how their emergence affected the democratic process. *The Causes of World War III* can be read as a jeremiad—a bitter lament—on Weber's ideas on the irrationality of many bureaucratic organizations, or as Mills called it, the disjunction between institutional rationality and human reason (or sometimes simply "crackpot realism"). Finally, *The Sociological Imagination* is an elaboration of the rationalization of social life and a plea for social scientists and intellectuals to identify and organize resistance to this trend. We will begin exploring this overarching theme of rationalization with a quick summation of some basic assumptions Mills has about the nature of man and society.

ASSUMPTIONS

Mills (1959/1976) began with the assumption that "human nature" is formed by the interaction of historical and social structure (p. 13). Sociocultural systems, in particular the modern nation-state, determine the type of men and women who inhabit those systems. Human beings, Mills asserted, cannot be understood apart from the social and historical structures in which they are formed and in which they interact (1959/1976, p. 162). The nation-state has become the "history-making unit" in the modern world, the "man-making unit" (Mills, 1959/1976, p. 158). Through the socialization process, aspects of human character are liberated or repressed. As the history-making unit, the nation-state selects and forms the character of human beings; it opens up possibilities and imposes limits on the variety of men and women who make up the society.

The struggle between countries or blocs of countries—such as occurred between fascism and democracy or between capitalism and communism—is to determine, not only which political or economic system will prevail, but also which types of human beings will prevail (Mills, 1959/1976, p. 158). Historical transformations within societies—such as the decline of agricultural jobs and the increase in sales and bureaucratic occupations—also affect the predominant character of human beings. By "predominant character" Mills means their values and ideologies, their beliefs and expectations. Again, men and women can only be understood in the context of the historical sociocultural system in which they live and interact.

While human beings are motivated by the norms, values, and belief systems that prevail in their society, structural change often throws these "vocabularies of motivation" into some confusion (Mills, 1959/1976, p. 162). As institutions become larger, more embracing, and more interconnected, the number and variety of structural changes within a society increase (Mills, 1959/1976, pp. 20–21). As structural institutions become enlarged and centralized, the circle of those who control these organizations also becomes narrowed (Mills, 1951/1973, p. 21). Consequently, the tempo of change has sped up appreciably in the modern era, and the changes have become far more consequential for all—for those who are in control of these enlarged organizations and for those who are subject to them.

BUREAUCRACY

According to Mills, the rise of white-collar work is rooted in occupational change due to (a) recent growth in bureaucracies, (b) technological change, and (c) the increasing need to market the goods of industrial society. This section will examine Mills's analysis of the effects of growing bureaucratization and technological change on the character of white-collar life. The section titled "Mass Society" will examine Mills's analysis of the long-range and pervasive impact of technological change and marketing on human behavior.

Through the expansion of production as well as mergers, corporations become larger, and many former "free entrepreneurs" become mere employees. With the growth of these large bureaucracies, increasing proportions of employees are needed to coordinate and manage others. These midlevel managers, in turn, report to supervisors and become the links in the "chains of power and obedience, coordinating and supervising other occupational experiences, functions and skills" (Mills, 1951/1973, p. 69). With the growth and bureaucratization of the corporate structure, the increasing tasks of government draw still more people into "occupations that regulate and service property and men" (Mills, 1951/1973, p. 69).

The central characteristics of white-collar workers in modern industrial societies are a lack of internal organization of their numbers and their dependence on large bureaucracies for their existence. Unlike the professionals of old, modern white-collar workers are not free to exercise professional judgment and control; rather, they are subject to the manipulations and control of the organization. By rising to numerical importance in the middle of the twentieth century, white-collar workers have upset the Marxist expectations that society would be divided between entrepreneurs and manual laborers. Their mass existence and dependence on bureaucracies for their livelihood have changed the character and feel of American life. Through a thorough examination of white-collar life, Mills believed, one can learn much about American character (Mills, 1951/1973, p. xv).

Mills repeatedly made the point that white-collar people are dependent upon the organization for their livelihood. To get and keep these jobs they sell, not only their time and skills, but also their personalities. This is because even the most personal traits are of relevance to the smooth functioning of the organization or to the marketing of goods and services. White-collar workers must learn to repress any resentment or aggression. They are required to smile and dance on command, to live at all times on the job in accordance with the rules of the organization laid down from above.

Mills identified the division of labor as permeating ever-higher reaches of the white-collar hierarchy. Jobs and tasks that used to be performed by a single individual are now broken up in terms of functions and parceled out to several. Many executives are becoming less autonomous, permitted less initiative on the job. Because of centralization, brought on by the thrust toward greater efficiency, decision making increasingly "becomes the application of fixed rules" (Mills, 1951/1973, p. 141).

This parceling out (or "industrialization") of many executive tasks has allowed bureaucracies to extend the reach of many professionals—allowing them to serve many more clients—through the proliferation of the "semi-professions" and office technology. The semi-professions consist of men and women of very specialized training who provide limited and circumscribed services, often under the supervision of the professional. Compared to the traditional professional, semi-professionals have limited authority, prestige, and income (Mills, 1951/1973, p. 141). It is to the semi-professions that the children of the working classes often aspire.

The other development that has enabled the ever more detailed division of labor is the new office machines. In 1951, Mills already saw the use of office automation as a prime mover in the drive toward centralization in the pursuit of efficiency and profits. And he saw that it was just the beginning. "Only when the machinery and the social organization of the office are fully integrated in terms of maximum efficiency per dollar spent will that age be full blown" (Mills, 1951/1973, p. 195).

Jobs, Mills observed, are broken up into simple functional tasks. Standards are set in terms of pace and output. Where economically viable, machines are employed. Where automation is impossible, the tasks are parceled out to the unskilled. Policy making and executive functions are centralized and moved up the hierarchy. Semi-professionals are employed to execute these decisions and keep the hierarchy informed. This increasing automation and hyper-specialization is done with an eye toward increasing output while lowering per unit costs, all of which is integral to the centralization and enlargement of executive authority, prestige, and wealth.

With the automation of the office and the growth in the division of labor, the number of routine jobs is increased, and authority and job autonomy become attributes of only the top positions. Greater distinctions are made in terms of power, prestige, and income between managers and staff (Mills, 1951/1973, p. 205). The routinized worker is discouraged from using his own independent judgment; his decision making is in accordance with strict rules handed down by others. He becomes alienated from his intellectual capacities, and work becomes an enforced activity. The worker is prevented from fully realizing himself in his work. By engaging in routinized activity in the name of efficiency, he is separated from the work process, estranged from the self (Mills, 1951/1973, p. 226).

Many of the trends in the workplace of the 1950s, Mills reported, served to undermine the status of the white-collar worker. Increasingly white-collar work is losing associated skills, autonomy, and thus prestige. One trend is the sheer growth in the number of white-collar jobs, which is serving to devalue their status. This growth is fueled by the increase in the number of people from the lower classes receiving a high school education. When everybody joins a club, Mills noted, it is no longer exclusive, no longer prestigious.[3] Other trends that serve to devalue white-collar work include (a) down-grading education and skill levels, (b) increasing rates of unemployment among such workers, and (c) the raising of the manual laborer's income. Mills believed this status decline has many effects on the character of the white-collar worker.

The increase in the number of white-collar workers also has a profound effect on educational systems in bureaucratic-industrial societies. Educated intelligence, in the traditional sense, becomes penalized in the workplace, where job performance and promotion are based on routinized work and following the bureaucratic rules and dictates of others (Mills, 1951/1973, p. 267). As a result, Mills said, American education has shifted toward a vocational focus. High schools, as well as colleges, have become the training grounds for the large bureaucracies of government and industry (1951/1973, p. 266).

The aim of a college education today is to prepare the young for a good job in a large corporation or for service in a government agency. This involves not only vocational training but also instruction in the proper social values, etiquette, and mannerisms (Mills, 1951/1973, p. 267). While the aim of nineteenth century American schooling was the creation of the "good citizen" of democracy, in the middle of the twentieth century it has become the making of the successful man or woman in a society of specialists.

POWER AND AUTHORITY

It is in *White Collar*, not *The Power Elite*, that Mills first noted the tremendous enlargement and centralization of bureaucracies in modern industrial societies. One consequence of this bureaucratic expansion, Mills asserted, is the sheer growth in the number of managers and administrators in every sphere of society. As with any position within the social structure, the position of manager or administrator prescribes a set of role expectations and behaviors. Mills labeled these role expectations the "managerial demiurge" (1951/1973, p. 77). Because the role of manager is so central to modern bureaucratic society, with such a

large number of people holding the position and many times more subject to their authority, the managerial demiurge has profound consequences for the society as a whole.

Mills identified three forms of power: (a) coercion or physical
force, (b) authority which is attached to positions and is often justified
by the beliefs of the obedient, and (c) manipulative power that is
wielded without the conscious knowledge of those subject to it (Mills,
1958, p. 41). While bureaucratic structures are based on authority relations, Mills saw many bureaucracies rapidly shifting toward manipulation as their primary means of exercising power.

Manipulation is not based on terror or external force, although the
police powers of the state undergird all forms of state authority. Human
organizations that depend on the constant use of force and intimidation
to discipline members are extremely inefficient and ultimately ineffec-
tive. A system based solely on force must expend much energy policing
its members; it stifles initiative, and it provides an obvious target for
rallying opposition (Mills, 1951/1973, p. 110). Rather, the power of
manipulation is founded upon the ever more sophisticated methods of
control provided by science (including social science) and technology.
In a society dominated by large bureaucracies, the truly efficient organization is based on the techniques and technologies of manipulation.

Mills characterized the managerial demiurge as an elaborate game
of manipulation based on both bureaucratic and political skills
(1951/1973, p. 81). As modern management becomes the reigning
ethos of the age, the preferred form of power shifts from explicit authority relationships to more subtle manipulation (Mills, 1951/1973, p.
106). The managerial demiurge does not stop at coordinating the simple behaviors of men and women under its sway—it extends to their
opinions and emotions as well (Mills, 1951/1973, p. 110).

The shift from authority to manipulation is enabled partly by new
technologies of mass communication and partly by new ideologies of
management and advances in the social sciences (Mills, 1951/1973, p.
110). However, these technological advances (and advances in tech-
nique) merely allow the change to occur. The cause of the shift is the
centralization and enlargement of political power itself. Authority
needs legitimation to secure loyalty and obedience. Manipulation arises
when such centralized authority is not publicly justified and when those
in power do not believe they can justify it (Mills, 1951/1973, pp. 349–
350).

The goal of manipulation is to have men and women internalize
managerial directives without knowing that these directives are not
their own motives, without recognizing that they are being victimized

(Mills, 1951/1973, p. 110). In the shift from coercion and authority to manipulation, power moves from the overt to the covert, from the obvious to the subtle. Exploitation becomes a psychological process (Mills, 1951/1973, p. 110).

Symbols of legitimation, Mills maintained, are among the most important areas of study for sociologists. These symbols serve to justify or to oppose the arrangements of power and authority within society. However, such symbols are not autonomous, as many claim. Governments do not necessarily rely on the consent of the governed. Governors can now manufacture consent. Sociologists must not confuse government's legitimations with its causes (Mills, 1959/1976, p. 37).

In precapitalist times, power and authority were obvious and personal, often engendering fear and obedience. If, however, that power should fail to keep people in line, the authority easily could become the target of revolt. Manipulative power, on the other hand, is soft and often disguised as therapeutic or advisory. Because manipulation is hidden, it deprives the oppressed from identifying the oppressor. Manipulative power effectively removes the check of reason and conscience of the ruled on the ruler (Mills, 1959/1976, pp. 40–41).

Over the years the United States has transformed from a nation of small capitalist enterprise to an economy dominated by large corporations. Yet the capitalist ideology of small businesses competing for contested markets persists and is used to justify the status quo (Mills, 1951/1973, p. 34). Religion is also used to bless and to legitimate the reigning power relationships. Rather than being used to guide men in the development of conscience, Mills asserted, religious leaders more often blunt that conscience and cover it up with "peace of mind" (1958, p. 152).

Large bureaucratic organizations also affect the relations between the rulers and the ruled. Such organizations insulate the managers from those in lower offices, cutting off those in the upper reaches of the hierarchy from identifying with those at the bottom (Mills, 1951/1973, pp. 110–111). In a bureaucratic setting the decision-maker is often far removed from his victims. Opposition in such a situation is difficult to organize. Because of manipulation, targets for revolt are not readily recognizable, and because of bureaucratization they are not readily available (Mills, 1951/1973, p. 349). Such a situation promotes not only schemers whose explicit ideology is to manipulate the ruled, but also a system of social control that fosters irresponsibility on the part of the rulers.

White-collar people subject to the manipulations and control of their superiors lose both freedom and creativity on the job. Many of these individuals will learn to seek satisfactions elsewhere (Mills, 1951/1973, p. 228). Emptied of all other meanings and legitimations, jobs have no intrinsic meaning. Money, in order to build a life outside of work, becomes the only rationale for work itself.

Human factors, such as personality and disposition, increasingly play a role in the efficiency and productivity of bureaucracies and service agencies. Because of this, human relations management has increasingly focused on morale (Mills, 1951/1973, p. 233). The object of this form of management is to give the workers the illusion of personal autonomy and of a caring environment in order to engender loyalty and commitment to the organization. Management thus becomes an elaborate manipulation of workers to maximize productivity (Mills, 1951/1973, p. 235).

ELITES

Mills believed that the bureaucratization of the social structure was partial and unevenly spread. Yet he saw it as an ongoing process, one that threatened to replace a loosely integrated democracy with a more managed "corporate-like society" (Mills, 1951/1973, p. 78). The technology of violence and the degree of organization that prevails in a society, Mills pointed out, have always limited the power of decision makers. However, in the West, the means of violence has greatly increased, and the degree of organization has enlarged, centralized, and become ever more efficient (Mills, 1956/1970, p. 23). Those at the top of the bureaucratic hierarchies that dominate modern industrial society are far more powerful than Caesar, Napoleon, Lenin, or even Hitler. "That the facilities of power are enormously enlarged and decisively centralized means that the decisions of small groups are now more consequential" (Mills, 1956/1970, p. 23).

According to Mills, modern societies have a power elite who command the resources of vast bureaucratic organizations that have come to dominate industrial societies (1956/1970, pp. 3–4). As the bureaucracies have centralized and enlarged, the circle of those who run these organizations has narrowed, and the consequences of their decisions have become enormous (Mills, 1956/1970, p. 7). According to Mills, the power elite are the key people in the three major institutions of modern society: (1) government, (2) military, and (3) corporations. Each of these areas has become larger, more powerful, and more centralized in its decision making. Together, the leaders of these institutions have become a unified elite who, while not omnipotent, are formidable.

The elite occupy key leadership positions within the bureaucracies that now dominate modern societies (Mills, 1956/1970, p. 9). Thus their power is rooted in authority, an attribute of social organizations, not of individuals. The bureaucracies of state, corporations, and the military have become enlarged and centralized and are a means of power never before equaled in human history. These hierarchies are crucial to understanding modern industrial societies, for they are the very basis of power, wealth, and prestige in modern times.

By asserting that there is a power elite in American society, Mills was not claiming that a self-conscious ruling class cynically manipulates the masses. It is not a conspiracy of evil men, he argued, but a social structure that has enlarged and centralized the decision-making process and then placed this authority in the hands of men of similar social background and outlook (Mills, 1956/1970, pp. 7–9). In Mills's view, major national power now resides almost exclusively in the economic, political, and military domains. All other institutions have diminished in scope and authority and have been pushed to the side of modern history or made subordinate to the big three.

For example, schools have become appendages of corporations and government, sorting and training young people for their corporate careers, and in so doing inculcating patriotism, respect for authority, and the glories of capitalism along the way. Families are still major socialization agents of the young, but they now share this function with schools and the mass media (1956/1970, p. 6). Through the socialization process, each person has come to embrace and internalize the system as it is. A general consensus of what is right and natural, good and just, valued and reviled is forged. The interests of the elites become the interests of everyone: They become internalized and legitimized.

Similar social class backgrounds provide one of the major sources of unity among the elite. The majority of them, Mills asserted, come from the upper third of the income and occupational pyramids. They are born of the same class, attend the same preparatory schools and Ivy League universities, join the same exclusive gentleman's clubs, and belong to the same organizations. They are closely linked through intermarriage. It is these common experiences and the role expectations of their positions that produce men of similar character and values (Mills, 1956/1970, p. 19). Non-upper-class members of the elite consist of hired corporate managers, experts, and corporate lawyers—competent technocrats who have risen through the ranks and are subsequently sponsored by the elite and the organizations that they control.

Mills contended that coordination between government and corporations does not just depend on private clubs or being from the same social class. Some of the coordination comes from the interchange of personnel between the three elite hierarchies. The closeness of business and government officials can be seen by the ease and frequency with which men pass from one hierarchy to another (Mills, 1951/1973, p. 83).

Mills also asserted that a good deal of the coordination comes from a growing structural integration of dominant institutions. As each of the elite domains becomes larger, more centralized, and more consequential in its activities, its integration with the other spheres becomes more pronounced, their decisions increasingly coordinated. An unstated structured bias develops of government and corporate leaders toward one another's interests. National governments are held accountable for the health of their economies. Economies rely on the production of military weapons and the projection of military power. There is an increasing convergence of the interests of the elite (Mills, 1956/1970, pp. 7–8). Of the three sectors of institutional power, Mills claimed, the corporate sector is the most powerful. But the power elite cannot be understood as a mere reflection of economic elites; rather, it is the alliance of economic, political, and military power.

Below the power elite, Mills identified two other levels of power in American society. At the bottom are the great masses of people. Largely unorganized, ill informed, and virtually powerless, they are controlled and manipulated from above. The masses are economically dependent and are economically and politically exploited. Because they are disorganized, the masses are far removed from the classic democratic public in which voluntary organizations hold the key to power (Mills, 1956/1970, pp. 28–29).

Between the masses and the elite Mills saw a middle level of power. Composed of local opinion leaders and special interest groups, this level neither represents the masses nor has any real effect on the elite. Mills believed the American Congress and political parties were a reflection of this middle level of power. Although Congress and political parties debate and decide some minor issues, the power elite ensures that no serious challenge to its authority and control is tolerated in the political arena (Mills, 1958, p. 36).

The liberal theory of government as the result of a moving balance of forces depends upon an assumption of truly independent units of roughly equal power. This assumption, according to Mills, rested upon the existence of a large and independent middle class. However, the old middle class declined with the small businessman, the true independent professional, and the family farm. A new class of white-collar workers and quasiprofessionals dependent upon large corporate, government, and military bureaucracies has replaced this old middle class. The new middle class is in the same economic position as the wage worker, dependent upon large organizations for their livelihood. Politically, they are in worse condition for they are not even represented by labor unions (Mills, 1958, p. 36).

The clash between competing interests occurs at the middle level of power, but it is mainly a conflict over a slice of the existing pie. Political commentators and political scientists write about this struggle, but it is far removed from any debate over fundamental policy. Even here, Mills asserted, the conflict among competing interests becomes muted as these interests increasingly become integrated into the apparatus of the state. Bureaucratic administration replaces politics, and the maneuvering of cliques replaces the open clash of parties.

The process of integrating previously autonomous political forces (such as labor, professional organizations, and farmers) into the modern state is overt in modern totalitarianism. Under such regimes independent organizations are co-opted and integrated as appendages of the state. In formal democracies the process is much less advanced and explicit, yet it is still well under way. These interest groups increasingly maneuver within and between the political parties and organs of the state, seeking to become a part of the state. Their chief desire is to maintain their organizations and to secure for their members maximum economic advantage (Mills, 1958, pp. 39–40). The middle level of power thus does not question the rule of the elite; nor does it seek any benefit for the great masses of men and women outside of their organization.

In those societies in which power is diffuse and decentralized, history is the result of innumerable decisions by numerous men. All contribute to eventual changes in social structure. In such societies, no one individual or small group has much control, and history moves "behind men's backs." However, in societies in which the means of power have become enlarged and centralized, those who control the dominant bureaucracies modify the structural conditions in which most people live; they have the means of affecting history (Mills, 1958, p. 22).

The positions of the elite allow them to transcend the environments of ordinary men and women. The elite have access to levers of power that make their decisions and actions (as well as their failure to act) consequential. In a society in which structural institutions have become enlarged, centralized, and all encompassing, who controls these institutions becomes the central issue. One important consequence of this fact, Mills asserted, is that leaders of the modern nation state can exert much more coordination and control over the actions of that state.

To date, Mills feared, these leaders are acting (or failing to act) with irresponsibility, thus leading the state and its citizens to disaster. However, this does not mean that it always must be so. The great structural change that has enlarged the means and extent of power and concentrated it in so few hands now makes it imperative to hold these men responsible for the course of events (Mills, 1958, p. 100).

With the publication of *The Causes of World War III* in 1958, Mills seemed much more concerned with the rise of militarism among the elites than with the hypothesis that many elites were military men. According to Mills (pp. 86–87), the rise of the military state serves the interests of the elite of industrial societies. For the politician the projection of military power serves as a cover for a lack of vision and innovative leadership. For corporate elites the preparations for war and the projection of military power underwrite their research and development and provide a guarantee of stable profits through corporate subsidies (Mills, 1958, p. 87). This militarism is inculcated in the population through schoolroom and pulpit patriotism, through manipulation and control of the news, through the cultivation of opinion leaders and unofficial ideology.

It is not just the existence of a power elite that has allowed this manufactured militarism to dominate. Militarism also has been enabled by the apathy and moral insensibility of the masses and by the political inactivity of intellectuals in both communist and capitalist countries. Most intellectual, scientific, and religious leaders echo the elaborate confusions of the elite. They refuse to question elite policies, they refuse to offer alternatives. They have abdicated their role, and they allow the elite to rule unhindered (Mills, 1958, pp. 88–89).

MASS SOCIETY

One of the great unifiers of life and character in the United States is the mass communications industry. Mass communications serve to mold modern consciousness and political thought (1951/1973, p. 333). Mills pointed out that there were no mass media to speak of in Marx's day, so its influence would be easy to overlook. But in the modern world, he asserted, the form and content of political and social consciousness cannot be understood without reference to the image of the world presented by these media.

What people come to believe about a whole range of issues is a function of their experience, their firsthand contact with others, and their exposure to the mass media. In this, Mills asserted, the media is often the decisive factor. The mass media are now the common denominator of American consciousness. They extend across all social environments, now even directly reaching out to mold the consciousness of children. Contents and images in the media have become a part of the American self-image and will over the next few generations modify the very character of human beings (Mills, 1951/1973, p. 334).

Mills was not writing simply of the news and the explicit political content of the mass media. This, he claimed, characterizes but a small portion of the fare served up to the American people on a daily basis. Rather, Mills focused on the rapidly growing entertainment and marketing industries. Entertainment and sports, which in their modern scale were only some 30 years old at Mills's writing, serve to divert attention from politics and social issues. The mass marketing of consumer products, which sponsor these attractions, is also a recent phenomenon that has a profound impact on the consciousness of men and women (Mills, 1951/1973, p. 336).

In an earlier era, salesmanship meant knowledge of a product and providing that information to the potential buyer. But the role of the salesman has shifted in a society that is threatened by a glut of consumer goods. Mass production has meant an increasing need to distribute goods to national markets. Now, with a constant need to move product, salesmanship focuses on "hypnotizing the prospect," a science/art pioneered by psychology that has become pervasive in society. Admen and psychologists attempt to improve their techniques of persuading people to buy (Mills, 1951/1973, p. 165).

Persuasion, according to Mills, becomes a style of life for all types of relationships—marketers selling their products, entrepreneurs selling their ideas, campaign managers selling their candidates, employees selling their selves. The culture of salesmanship has become so ingrained in the American psyche that it has become an "all-pervasive atmosphere," turning America into the "biggest bazaar" in the history of the world (Mills, 1951/1973, pp. 165–166). This "Big Bazaar," Mills asserted, is as important in understanding modern life as the family or the factory. Like the family, it feeds, clothes, and amuses, supplying all necessities and creating additional "needs." Like the factory, it manufactures the "dreams of life," dedicated to surrounding people with the "commodities for which they live" (Mills, 1951/1973, p. 167). Although success has always been a driving force in American society, the confusion of success with mere consumption has made it a "dubious motive," and emptied it of real meaning as a way of life (Mills, 1951/1973, p. 259).

RATIONALIZATION

What is at the root of the enlargement and centralization of structural bureaucracies in the modern world? Mills answered this question clearly and repeatedly: The rationalization of the world is the master trend of the twentieth century and beyond. The key to power in the modern world is social organization and technological development. The means of production are now structured to maximize efficiency, and in that cause bureaucracies have become ever more encompassing, work ever more alienating, and culture ever more exploitive. Also behind the growth in the power, scope, and scale of bureaucracy is the new technology of coordination and control—a technology that Mills recognized as being in its infancy (1951/1973, p. 195; 1956/1970, p. 7).

As applied to work in industrial-bureaucratic societies, rationalization has led to jobs that have been reduced to standardized (and thus easily repeatable) movements and decision making in accordance with written rules and regulations. Although rationalization has led to the unprecedented increase in both the production and distribution of goods and services, it is also associated with depersonalization, a loss of personal control over the work tasks, and oppressive routine.

The process of rationalization is not restricted to the office; it permeates all areas of social life. "Training for rationalization" begins in the school systems, as schools have been enjoined to provide job training, socialization into authority and bureaucracy, specialization, and goal-oriented problem solving. "Families as well as factories, leisure as well as work, neighborhoods as well as states—they become parts of a functionally rational totality" (Mills, 1959/1976, p. 169).

For example, Mills saw American farmers being rapidly polarized into two groups. The first he characterized as small subsistence farmers and wage workers; the second, as big commercial farmers and rural corporations (1951/1973, p. 19). Behind this movement toward ever increasing farm size or consequent bankruptcy, of course, stood the machine. The world of the corporate farmer is becoming more and more interdependent with the world of finance, business, and government. These bureaucracies carry the rationalization of the farm forward (Mills, 1951/1973, pp. 40–41).

Although Mills recognized that the rationalization of the farm had a ways to go before it was complete, it had already destroyed the rural way of life. Farming, he wrote, was becoming more and more like any other industry, the "family farm" a nostalgic term used to provide an "ideological veil" for large business interests (Mills, 1951/1973, p. 44).

Science in the United States, Mills pointed out, is another extremely rationalized and bureaucratized enterprise. From the start, science in America has been identified closely with its technological products and its techniques. Recently, it has taken on the social organization of the "assembly line." The United States has excelled especially in applied military and commercial projects and in the marketing and mass production of these discoveries and inventions. This is in stark contrast to the classic academic tradition of pure research, unfettered and uncoordinated by practical needs or commercial interests. "In brief, the U.S. has built a Science Machine: a corporate organization and rationalization of the process of technological development and to some extent—I believe unknown—of scientific discovery itself" (Mills, 1958, p. 161).

SOCIAL PROBLEMS

Mills's sociology focuses on substantive social problems of modern industrial societies. He identified five overarching problems:

1. alienation,
2. moral insensibility,
3. threats to democracy,
4. threats to human freedom, and
5. the conflict between bureaucratic rationality and human reason.

Each of these problems, according to Mills, is due to the bureaucratization/rationalization process.

Like Marx, Mills viewed the problem of alienation as a characteristic of modern society, one that is deeply rooted in the character of work. The shift from a rural and agriculturally based world to an urban society in which many employees depend upon large bureaucracies has created the "property conditions" for alienation to spread beyond the factory (Mills, 1951/1973, p. 224). Many of the characteristics of white-collar work are just as alienating as the manufacturing work that Marx wrote about. Most white-collar jobs do not entail much freedom or decision making on the job, and few entail work as craftsmanship.

White-collar work may be considered even more alienating than traditional blue-collar work, according to Mills (1951/1973, pp. 225, 227), because white-collar often involves the subjugation of the entire personality into the work process, not just the physical actions of the worker. This "personality market" that is part of much white-collar work "underlies the all-pervasive distrust and self-alienation so characteristic" of modern people (Mills, 1951/1973, pp. 87–88).[4]

However, Mills did not attribute alienation to capitalism alone. Although he argued that much alienation is due to the ownership of the means of production, he believed much of it is also due to the detailed division of labor (Mills, 1951/1973, p. 225). The precise degree of alienation will vary, according to Mills, with the degree of autonomy, freedom, and level of skill that a worker brings to the job. Nevertheless, almost any job in modern society will be characterized by some degree of alienation because the employee's actions are subject to the management of others.

Because of the detailed division of labor, the worker does not carry through the work process to the final product. In fact, the employee is often not even aware of the entire process. This, Mills argued, cut the link of meaning between process and product. White-collar work is also alienating because, even in many professional jobs, the workers are often denied the chance to employ their minds by the centralized decision making that characterizes the modern bureaucratic enterprise. The root cause of alienation, Mills stated, goes far beyond ownership and markets—it is in the form of organization itself. It is an organization that removes the workers from any understanding of their work, removes them from control over their work, and determines when and how fast they will work.

But modern workers do not feel the destruction of freedom, craftsmanship, and autonomy on the job as a crisis. They might feel it as a threat, Mills stated, if they had directly experienced the shift themselves or perhaps indirectly experienced it through their parents. However, this has not been the case. The loss has occurred gradually over the last several generations, so it is only in the imaginations of the social scientist that its importance can be gauged (Mills, 1951/1973, p. 228). However, even though American workers do not feel this loss of connection in their work, they are still disconnected. Such employees must seek meaning in their lives elsewhere.

One of the fundamental problems of mass society is that many people have lost their faith in leaders and are therefore very apathetic; they pay little attention to politics. Mills characterized such apathy as a "spiritual condition" that is at the root of many contemporary problems

(1958, pp. 81–82). For example, war and peace between nations, Mills claimed, cannot be understood through naïve appeals to better communications between people or assertions of innate human aggression. War in modern times, Mills wrote, is rooted in the apathy of the people who are "selected, molded, and honored in the mass society"; this leads to "moral insensibility" (1958, p. 81). Such people mutely accept atrocities committed by their leaders. They lack indignation when confronted with moral horror, and they lack the capacity to morally react to the character, decisions, and actions of their leaders (Mills, 1958, p. 82).

Mass communications contribute to this condition, Mills argued, through the sheer volume of images aimed at the individual in which she "becomes the spectator of everything but the human witness of nothing" (1958, p. 83). Images of horror become commonplace. Atrocities are gotten used to; they are emptied of any human meaning. There is little sense of moral outrage or shock.

Mills related this moral insensibility directly to the rationalization process. Acts of cruelty and barbarism are split from human consciousness—both perpetrators and observers. People perform these acts as part of their roles in formal organizations. They are guided not by individual consciousness, but by the orders of others. Thus many actions are inhuman, not because of the scale of their cruelty, but because they are impersonal, efficient, and performed without any real emotion (Mills, 1958, pp. 83–84). People no longer recognize any inner moral constraint; the only constraints to their actions (and the actions of leaders) come from outside—fear of reprisal from more powerful entities or simple political expediency.

Mills believed that widespread alienation, political indifference, and economic and political concentration of power are serious threats to democracy. Mills defined democracy as simply a system in which those who are affected by decisions have an effective voice in those decisions. According to Mills, six conditions are essential for maintaining a modern democratic state:

1. a public that is both informed of issues and actively involved in debating these issues;
2. "nationally responsible parties" that debate these issues clearly and openly;
3. a skilled civil service independent of any private or corporate interests;
4. intellectuals, both within and outside of academe, who carry on work truly relevant to public policy;

5. a mass media of communication that is informed by these debates and is capable of translating issues to a broader public; and

6. free associations that are capable of linking individuals, families, communities and publics with more formal organizations such as corporations, the military, and agencies of government (Mills, 1958, pp. 121–123).

As is apparent, Mills considered discussion and debate as the cornerstone of democracy. Free associations are necessary vehicles for the exercise and formation of reasoned options. Further, these associations are necessary to prepare people for leadership at all levels in a free democratic society (Mills, 1958, p. 123). There were a number of discrepancies between Mills's conception of an ideal modern democratic state and what was occurring in America. Because of these discrepancies, Mills pointed out, small groups and associations are in decline, and those that do discuss important issues have only "a faint and restraining voice" in formal decision making (1958, p. 123).

The structural factor that prevents the fulfillment of the six conditions for democracy, however, is the existence of a power elite in American society. Private corporations acting in their own interests, the ascendancy of militarism, and the refusal of government to address either one are key factors in the decline of democracy in America (Mills, 1958, pp. 123–124). Power in America is concentrated in a handful of huge bureaucratic organizations. The lines of control between the powerful at the top of these organizations and any democratic control—even among agencies of government itself—"become blurred and tenuous" (Mills, 1951/1973, p. 158).

Mills saw America as a society of privatized men dominated by huge bureaucratic organizations. These organizations have not been firmly legitimized, and they do not engender widespread loyalty or enthusiasm. However, Mills did not see society as being in any danger of imminent collapse. A society held together by convention and a network of bureaucratic power, he argued, even if only lightly legitimated, may last many years. This is particularly true if the society can deliver high levels of material goods and comfort (Mills, 1951/1973, pp. 350–351).

Finally, Mills was continually concerned in his writings with the threat to two fundamental human values: freedom and reason. Mills characterized the trends that imperil these values as being "co-extensive with the major trends of contemporary society" (1959/1976, pp. 129–130). These trends are, Mills stated throughout his writings, the centralization and enlargement of vast bureaucratic organizations and the placing of extraordinary power and authority into the hands of a small elite.

Economic security used to be based on property ownership. For many, however, economic concentration has shifted the basis of economic security to employment. Because employees by definition are dependent upon bureaucracy for their economic security—a bureaucracy over which they have little control—they can be neither truly free nor secure (Mills, 1951/1973, pp. 58–59). Because of the concentration of wealth and power, economic freedom—the freedom to do with one's property what one wishes—now places the economic security of thousands of dependent employees at risk, and thus places their freedom at risk as well.

For the individual, rational organization is an alienating organization, destructive of freedom and autonomy. It cuts the individual off from the conscious conduct of her behavior, thought, and ultimately emotions. The individual is guided in her actions not by her consciousness, but by the prescribed roles and the rules of the organization itself.

> It is not too much to say that in the extreme development the chance to reason of most men is destroyed, as rationality increases and its locus, its control, is moved from the individual to the big-scale organization. There is then rationality without reason. Such rationality is not commensurate with freedom but the destroyer of it. (Mills, 1959/1976, p. 170)

In the eighteenth and nineteenth centuries, Mills pointed out, the steady emergence of society organized along rational and democratic principles appeared to be at the forefront of human liberation. The irrationalities of traditional monarchies or the rule of the strong and the ruthless increasingly were seen as antithetical to liberty and human happiness.

> Now rationality seems to have taken on a new form, to have its seat not in individual men, but in social institutions which by their bureaucratic planning and mathematical foresight usurp both freedom and rationality from the little individual men caught in them. (Mills, 1951/1973, p. xvii)

It is these "calculating hierarchies" that now lay out the "gray ways" of work that circumscribe individual autonomy and initiative.

Like Weber before him, Mills cautioned that a society dominated by rational social organization is not based on reason, intelligence, and good will toward all. Weber summarized this as the difference between substantive (holistic) and formal (bureaucratic) rationality, claiming that the two are often in conflict. In that same vein, Mills asserted that a society dominated by bureaucratic rationality is not one based upon the summation of all the constituent individuals' capacity to reason. He further stated that bureaucratic rationality often serves to prevent individuals from even acquiring that capacity (Mills, 1958, p. 175; 1959/1976, p. 169). It is through rational social organization that modern-day tyrants (as well as more mundane bureaucratic managers) exercise their authority and manipulation, often denying their subjects opportunity to exercise their own judgments. Therefore, Mills argued, as a social product, the human mind might well be deteriorating in quality and cultural level (1959/1976, p. 175).

ROLE OF SOCIAL SCIENCE

One of the central conditions for a modern democracy to exist, according to Mills, is a vibrant intellectual community that is involved intimately in providing knowledge and wisdom to help guide decisions of social polity. By "intellectual community," Mills was referring to scientists, ministers, scholars, artists, and students, those who are part of the great Western tradition of reason beginning with the Greeks (1958, p. 129). The intellectual community, through art, speech, and writing create and disseminate ideas and images that focus the attention of publics on relevant or irrelevant issues and justifies or criticizes the policies of those in authority (Mills, 1958, p. 129).

The dissemination of publicly relevant ideas by the intellectual community is vital because private experience enables each individual to "know only a small portion of the social world, only a few of the decisions that now affect them" (Mills, 1958, p. 173). The significant problems of contemporary society are intricate, but they are not so complex that only professionals and experts can deal with them. The central task of the intellectual is to confront these complications and make social issues accessible to public understanding, discussion, and debate (Mills, 1958, p. 15). Democracy requires that publics affected by decisions are knowledgeable about the issues. Only through the intellectual community fulfilling its task can society bring reason to bear on social issues and can democracy be more than a sham.

If intellectuals fail to confront these issues, Mills continually asserted, they are in default of their intellectual heritage and have abdicated their duty to society (1951/1973, p. 158). What scientist, Mills asked, can claim to be part of the legacy of the great Western scientific tradition and yet work for the Military Industrial Complex? What social scientist can claim to be part of the legacy of Western humanism and, despite a world in which "reason and freedom" are under attack, retreat into methodologically sophisticated studies of trivia? What minister can know God and still approve of the immorality and irresponsibility of leaders? Unfortunately, Mills concluded, many in the intellectual community are in default (1958, p. 130).

If they are in default, if they fail to speak out as public men and women, intellectuals contribute to the erosion of human freedom, dignity, and democracy (Mills, 1958, p. 170). Worse, in Mills's view, are members of the intellectual community who provide misleading images of the elite as men of reason who are acting in national as opposed to private interests. Such images serve to "soften the political will," allowing men to accept the irresponsibility and greed "without any sense of outrage." Such apologists allow the elite to escape any accountability to the public, essentially giving "up the central goal of Western humanism, so strongly felt in nineteenth-century American experience: the audacious control by reason of man's fate" (Mills, 1958, p. 173).

As early as *White Collar* in 1951, Mills was decrying the excessive specialization of the professorate. Such hyperspecialization leads to an inability to think outside of one's narrowly defined area (Mills, 1951/1973, pp. 130–131). The prestige system of the academy, of course, contributes to this trend. Books that attempt to span more than one specialty are frowned upon, as are the general textbooks within a field. Instead, academic honor and prestige are given for massive tomes on narrow subjects.

This narrowing of knowledge is furthered in the social sciences and humanities by aping the methods of the natural sciences—methods that are particularly suited for studying "microscopic fields of inquiry, rather than expanding it to embrace man and society as a whole" (Mills, 1951/1973, p. 131).

Like other institutions in society, the university is becoming more and more bureaucratic. This organization has similar effects on the professorate, other professionals, and businessmen. It turns all into bureaucrats executing specialized tasks in accordance with the rules and regulations of the institution (Mills, 1951/1973, p. 138). The bureaucratic nature of colleges and universities—the hierarchy of authority, the middle-class environment, the separation of intellectual and social life, the excessive academic specialization—contributes to conformity of thought.

The same trends that limit independence of intellect in the larger society are present on the university campus. The professor is an em-

ployee and like all employees is subject to the rule from above in terms
of the conditions of work. Writing in the early 1950s, of course, Mills
noted the attempts to restrain academic freedom through political intimidation of professors. However, he described such attacks as overtly
affecting only a few. Their purpose is in setting the tone for more subtle
control of the professorate. Whereas some outright intimidation occurs
on some university campuses brought about through tenure, promotion,
and merit procedures, there is also the more subtle pressure of collegial
control of potential "insurgents." Such pressures keep professors in
conformance through "agreements of academic gentlemen" (Mills,
1951/1973, pp. 151–152). These subtle controls on academic life also
are furthered by political and business attempts to standardize curricu-
lums and by the granting or denial of research funds from government
agencies and foundations that are "notably averse" to scholars outside
the mainstream (Mills, 1951/1973, pp. 151–152).

The first and central task of the social sciences, according to Mills,
is to develop a comprehensive framework for understanding humans
and society. This theoretical viewpoint should be simple enough to
allow nonspecialists to understand, yet comprehensive enough to encompass the full range and variety of human behavior (Mills,
1959/1976, p. 133). In accomplishing this task, Mills's outlook was
decidedly interdisciplinary. Whereas each of the social sciences tends
to specialize in a particular institutional order, any mature social science will relate its findings to the other institutional domains as well.
Further, any social science worthy of the name, according to Mills, is
firmly rooted in history (1959/1976, pp. 145–146).

The problem with much social science today, according to Mills's
view, is that it is devoid of both theory and any sense of history. Being
atheoretical, the social scientist often overlooks the relationships
among various technologies, structures, and ideas. Being ahistorical,
many social scientists lack the ability to recognize new trends as well
as to discriminate between trends of major and minor significance.
Classical social analysis, Mills repeatedly insisted, consists of a set of
usable traditions and insights that are strongly rooted in history and
theory (1959/1976, p. 21).

Classical social science also focuses on substantive social problems. It neither builds up from empirical observation nor does it begin
with a grand theory of sociocultural systems and deduce down to human behavior. Rather, classic social science places empirical research
and theory building in a continuous interaction. Practitioners of the
craft attempt to develop comprehensive frameworks for understanding
social order, social change, and social problems. They then continually

test and reformulate these explanatory frameworks in light of empirical study (Mills, 1959/1976, p. 128).

However, trends within the social sciences as well as in the broader society are endangering the classical tradition and stand in the way of greater social understanding (Mills, 1959/1976, p. 21). Mills maintained that three different styles of doing social science serve to obscure rather than increase people's understanding of human social behavior: abstracted empiricism, grand theory, and the use of social science to improve bureaucratic efficiency.

Of the three styles, Mills's identification of grand theory and his critique of it now appear dated. His problem with grand theory was really with the work of Talcott Parsons. Mills took Parsons to task for his (rather painful) elaboration and clarification of concepts, and his alleged inability to apply this generalized theory to further understanding of more concrete reality. Parsons's type of theory proved to be a short-term trend in the social sciences. Grand theory as defined by Mills is not a widespread practice in any of the social sciences today. However, the other two styles in the social sciences identified by Mills, abstracted empiricism and the use of data to address bureaucratic problems of coordination and control, now dominate.

Abstracted empiricism is the reification of method and methodology above the substance of the discipline. Sociologists become the masters in the techniques of research and then use their surveys and other instruments to collect facts on almost any social phenomenon. According to Mills, a certain mystique has grown up around the use of sophisticated research methods, a mystique that is misplaced. Much of social research is rather "thin and uninteresting." It provides useful exercises for students, gives employment to unimaginative social scientists, but has nothing in it inherently superior to other types of scholarship (Mills, 1959/1976, p. 205). The purpose of empirical research, he asserted, should be simply to discipline ideas (Mills, 1959/1976, p. 71).

By far the greatest threat to the fulfillment of the promise of the social sciences, however, is the co-optation of the craft by bureaucracy. Increasingly, the huge bureaucracies that dominate modern life are using social science (and social scientists) to extend their control. Social scientists are often employed by the military, by social service agencies, by the criminal justice system, and by corporations (Mills, 1959/1976, p. 80). Experts in "human relations" for example, are working to improve the morale of employees. They are engaged in "manipulation," defining "morale" and exploring ways to improve that morale within the existing relationships of power and authority (Mills, 1959/1976, pp. 94–95). Social scientists who work for such bureaucracies are more concerned with administrative problems than human problems, more concerned with efficiency than with humanity. Social science in this cause—whether it be for the military, the advertising agency, or the government bureau—is social science for the "non-democratic areas of society" (Mills, 1959/1976, pp. 114–115). The goal of such research is simply to make bureaucracies more efficient, which therefore not only distracts social scientists from their essential task, but also supports the powerful and the status quo (Mills, 1959/1976, p. 117).

Values, according to Mills, necessarily affect social research. They certainly play a role in selecting the problems that social scientists study as well as many "key conceptions." However, the social scientist should be very clear and explicit about her values and then should strive to avoid bias in her work (Mills, 1959/1976, p. 78).[5] Mills held a similar view in regard to teaching. The professor should strive to be very explicit in terms of the assumptions and judgments that he makes. He should clearly indicate to his students "the full range of moral alternatives," and then make his own choices known (Mills, 1959/1976, p. 79).

THE SOCIOLOGICAL IMAGINATION

In *White Collar*, Mills took an initial stab at defining the sociological imagination by calling it "the first lesson of modern sociology." To understand experience, Mills asserted, people must locate that experience within the context of historical time and within social strata (1951/1973, p. xx). Whether people believe it or not, Mills wrote, historical and economic forces move people. Such forces are the stuff of sociology. Ordinary men and women often are oblivious to these forces in their lives, or they may be only dimly aware of their impact (Mills, 1959/1976, p. 3).

The sociological imagination is simply a "quality of mind" that allows one "to grasp history and biography and the relations between the two within society" (Mills, 1959/1976, p. 6). The sociological imagination enables one to switch from one perspective to another, thereby forming a comprehensive view of the sociocultural system (Mills, 1959/1976, p. 211). This quality of mind is characteristic of the best of classical social analysis—it is why much of it is still so useful in understanding social reality. It is also characteristic of the best in social science today (Mills, 1959/1976, p. 6).

Social scientists who employ the sociological imagination in their work consistently address structural and historical issues, and how these issues affect human values and behavior. Structurally, imaginative analysts examine the various components of sociocultural systems and how they relate to one another. Such analysts also compare and contrast the components of differing sociocultural systems. Historically, the imaginative researcher looks at the major historical trends that affect society through time, she examines the mechanics of social trends and change, and she compares the society to itself over different historical times (Mills, 1959/1976, pp. 6–7). Most important, the social scientist of imagination asks how these structures and history have formed and shaped the members of the sociocultural system. "What varieties of men and women now prevail in this society and in this period? And what varieties are coming to prevail"? (Mills, 1959/1976, p. 7).

To truly fulfill the promise of the discipline, sociologists must focus upon substantive problems and relate them to structural and historical features of the sociocultural system. Social structure and history have meanings for individuals, and they profoundly affect the values, character, and behavior of the men and women who make up that sociocultural system (Mills, 1959/1976, p. 134).

The social sciences are often used in "ideological ways." They are used in legitimating power, in criticizing or debunking the powerful, and in distracting attention away from meaningful issues (Mills, 1959/1976, p. 80). The promise of the social sciences is to bring reason to bear on human affairs (Mills, 1959/1976, p. 193). To fulfill this role requires that social scientists "avoid furthering the bureaucratization of reason and of discourse" (Mills, 1959/1976, p. 192). In C. Wright Mills's own words,

> What I am suggesting is that by addressing ourselves to issues and to troubles, and formulating them as problems of social science, we stand the best chance, I believe the only chance, to make reason democratically relevant to human affairs in a free society, and so to realize the classic values that underlie the promise of our studies. (1959/1976, p. 194)

EXCURSUS: MODERN AMERICAN BUREAUCRACY

How large and pervasive are bureaucracies in America today? How much power do they wield? One possible measure for the size of capitalist bureaucracies is the amount of economic resources controlled by a single organization. On this measure they are very powerful indeed. Thomas Dye has written a series of books (one every four years or so) that attempt to empirically gauge the concentration of power in American society. In 2000 Dye summarized that

> Economic power in America is highly concentrated. Indeed, only about 4,300 individuals—two-one-thousandths of 1 percent of the population—exercise formal authority over more than one half of the nation's industrial assets, two thirds of all banking assets, one half of all assets in communications and utilities, and more than two thirds of all insurance assets. These individuals are the presidents, officer-directors, and directors of the largest corporations in these fields. The reason for this concentration of power in the hands of so few people is found in the concentration of industrial and financial assets in a small number of giant corporations. (p. 15)

The amount of economic concentration reported by Dye is astounding. He reports, for example, that in 1990 there were about 200,000 industrial corporations in the United States with total assets of about $2.6 trillion. The largest 100 industrial corporations controlled about 75 percent of these assets. Dye also provides evidence that this concentration of resources among the top 100 industrials has increased over time, starting at 39.8 percent in 1950 (when Mills was writing), rising to 58.2 percent by 1983, and reaching 74.6 percent in 1992 (p. 15). It is no doubt even higher today. Dye finds even more concentration in communications and utilities, commercial banking (the largest 50 banks out of some 12,000 control 62 percent of all banking assets), and insurance (the largest 50 insurance companies out 2,200 control 81 percent of all assets) (pp. 16–20).

Government growth and centralization in the twentieth century is also well documented. Total employment in U.S. governments (all levels) has increased throughout the twentieth century. Another measure of government power is the percent of GDP spent by government. Again, the trends have risen dramatically in the twentieth century.

Mills never argued that it was all common social class, back-room deals, and explicit coordination among the elites. Rather he saw that a good part of the coordination came from a growing structural integration of the dominant institutions—corporate, military, and government—within society (Mills 1956/1970, pp. 7–8). Consider the use of the U.S. military in defending national interests abroad. The fact that most military hardware and supplies as well as increasing amounts of military services (food, transportation, security) are purchased from capitalist enterprise gives private industry a strong interest in promoting military spending. Since spending on the military provides employment, profit to powerful elites, and enables the nation to project power overseas, the American government has an interest in higher military spending as well. Because of this inherent interest, a view of the world that sees enemies everywhere is congruent with elite interests as well. Finally, the availability of such a marvelous tool as the American military to government officials may well lead them to (too) readily use this military to advance their perceived national interests.[6] They could be especially prone to the use of such power if their lives, or the lives of their close kin or friends, are not directly put at risk in the use of this power. The fact that the United States has intervened in the internal affairs of foreign nations hundreds of times in the twentieth century—far more than any other nation—gives credence to the view that such militarism is in the interests of both corporate and government elites.[7]

It is probable that Mills's focus on elites has somewhat obscured the issue of who rules America. Too often political scientists, sociologists, and historians look for explicit coordination—secret or not so secret meetings of the wealthy where they coordinate their activities, revolving doors between government and corporate boardrooms, and personal wealth being used directly to purchase access and position. While a good deal of this goes on, it is often difficult to document and is misleading in terms of the essential problem of a society dominated by huge bureaucratic organizations. The problem goes well beyond supposed communication and coordination between elites in these organizations. American government, even when not under the direct influence of elites who represent their class interests, will follow corporate priorities.

ABOUT MILLS

Charles Wright Mills was born August 28, 1916, in Waco, Texas. His father, Charles Grover Mills, was a salesman for an insurance company, which meant that he was often on the road. His mother, Frances Ursula Wright, was by all accounts a strong Catholic and attempted to raise her son in the same manner. She was not successful in this attempt. Until the age of 7, Mills lived in Waco, but then his family began frequently moving around Texas. According to Mills, his childhood was not a happy one.[7] In autobiographical writings (written in 1957) he described his early family life as one of isolation and loneliness, his father traveling for weeks at a time, a weak tie with his mother, no close siblings or real friends. "In grammar school and high school and college—in fact until my first marriage—I never had a circle of friends. There was for me no 'gang,' no parties" (Mills, 2000, p. 28).

In contrast to the early life of many academics, Mills's was not one steeped in culture or learning:

> I grew up in houses that had no books and no music in them. At least the only music I remember ever hearing in the house was a hillbilly version of "How You Gonna Keep 'Em Down on the Farm?" and I was in the second year of college when I first heard classical music. (Mills, 2000, p. 28)

In fact, Mills did not even remember reading much until his senior year in high school when he "suddenly became awake for the first time," reading some success books his father borrowed to improve his salesmanship.

In 1934–1935 Mills attended Texas A&M College (now University). It was a disastrous year. At that time Texas A&M was a strict, regimented school, with students required to wear uniforms and upperclassmen frequently demanding obedience and deference from the freshmen.[8] He recalled one incident:

> I was reading when three heads appeared in the door. "How do you do," I said. "What the hell do you mean—listen bastard, when sophomores walk in this god damned room, you get up. When juniors pass by, you get up damned quick, and when you see a senior a block off, get up and stay up until they're a block past—now get up." Then the three beat my butt. (Mills cited in Judas, 2001, para. 12)

Later that year Mills allegedly broke an opponent's arm during a wrestling match, after which he was completely excluded from campus life for the remainder of the year, receiving the silent treatment from all but one professor. In retaliation, Mills wrote letters to the *Battalion*, the campus newspaper, in which he attacked the class system of the school.

> What effect has the overbearing attitude of the upperclassman on the mind of the freshman? Does it make the freshman more of a man? Most assuredly not, for there can be no friendship born out of fear, hatred or contempt; and no one is a better man who submits passively to the slavery of his mind and body by one who is less of a man than he. (Mills, 2000, p. 31)

Again in 1957, Mills reflected on how these childhood and adolescent experiences affected his adult life. He concluded that they caused him to focus on his work as his "very salvation." His experiences taught him to rely on himself, to demand intellectual and social independence. He admitted that it also gave him some problems in forming deep and long-lasting relationships with others; not only did his experiences give him a tolerance for isolation, they also gave him a taste for it (Mills, 2000, pp. 31–34). These self-reflections appear to be fairly accurate.

The following year he transferred to the University of Texas where he became an exceptional student, earning a bachelor's degree in sociology and a master's degree in philosophy in 1939. At the University of Texas Mills studied the works of George Herbert Mead, Thorstein Veblen, William James, and John Dewey. In his last year at the university he published "Language, Logic and Culture" in the *American Sociological Review* and another article in the *American Journal of Sociology*, the preeminent journals in the field. In 1939 he went to the University of Wisconsin where he studied Weber under the German scholar, Hans Gerth. According to Horowitz (1983), Mills's experiences at Wisconsin did not endear him to his professors. He was looked on as arrogant and exceedingly ambitious. "With the exception of Gerth, Mills's professional relationships at Wisconsin were exceedingly argumentative and adversarial" (Horowitz, 1983, p. 51). Mills delighted in criticism of senior professors and friends alike. At the oral defense of his dissertation, he refused to make the changes that his committee asked for. "The defense became a standoff, and the dissertation was quietly accepted without ever being formally approved" (Horowitz, 1983, p. 53).

Mills's first academic position was at the University of Maryland in 1941. It was here that Mills finished his dissertation on American pragmatism and continued his collaboration (at a distance) with Hans Gerth.[8] The first fruit of this collaboration was a translation of Weber, *From Max Weber: Essays in Sociology* (1946). At the time, the major English translator of Weber was Talcott Parsons, the Harvard sociologist. Mills did not think much of his work, writing in a letter to a friend, "The son of a bitch translated it [a section of *Wirtschaft and Gesellschaft*] so as to take all the guts, the radical guts, out of it, whereas our translation doesn't do that!" (Mills, 2000, p. 53). Talcott Parsons ended up writing a glowing review of *From Max Weber*.

The second major collaboration Mills had with Gerth was *Character and Social Structure: The Psychology of Social Institutions* (1953), which centered on how the twentieth century's historic transformations in government, the economy, the military, and the family have affected the character and personalities of those living in society. Both books were well received. *Character and Social Structure* acknowledged the help of Robert Merton for a careful reading of the manuscript and contained a glowing foreword by Merton as well. In this and other early work, Mills was much in the forefront of mainstream academic sociology.

In 1945 he joined the Columbia University Labor Research Division of the Bureau of Applied Social Research at the invitation of Paul Lazarsfeld and Robert Merton. From his work at the institute *The New Men of Power*, a book about labor leaders, appeared in 1948. In 1946 he became an assistant professor at Columbia, and advanced to full professor status in 1956.

While at Columbia Mills began to write for an audience broader than professional sociologists. In a letter to his parents in December of 1946 Mills told them,

> This white collar book, ah, there's a book for the people; it is everybody's book. So I am trying to make it damn good all over. Simple and clean cut in style, but with a lot of implications and subtleties woven into it.... It is all about the new little man in the big world of the 20th century. It is about that little man and how he lives and what he suffers and what his chances are going to be; and it is also about the world he lives in, has to live [in], doesn't want to live in. It is, as I said, going to be everybody's book. For, in truth, who is not a little man. (Mills, 2000, p. 101)

As Mills's popularity grew around the world he became increasingly isolated as a sociologist. Part of this isolation was because he was writing increasingly for a broader audience, a singular sin in a profession that was in the process of both specialization and professionalization. *The Power Elite* was harshly criticized in the academic press, and *The Sociological Imagination* even more so. *The Causes of World War III* and other works after that, on the other hand, were viewed as mere journalism, increasingly strident and critical of the status quo. Then, there was the "professional sin" of freely criticizing immediate colleagues in public forums and in print. In *The Sociological Imagination*, Mills took on Paul Lazarsfeld for his "abstracted empiricism." His biographer, Irving Horowitz (1983, p. 83), believes that a good deal of the controversy Mills stirred up in sociology was due to his abrasive personality and personal style rather than any of his writing. Mills loved to play the role of the rebel, riding his BMW motorcycle, his personal manners and dress far removed from the buttoned-down academics of Columbia. In 1963 Mills died at the age of 45, virtually ex-communicated from his profession.[9]

NOTES

1. Apparently, his writing style was learned in his first years as a professor as a result of much practice. In "Mills at Maryland," William Form had this to say about Mills's acquisition of the craft: "Mills wrote a paper that he circulated prior to the faculty seminar. When we discussed it, Joslyn [Mills's department chair at Maryland, Carl S. Joslyn] raised several points for clarification. Mills was mystified by the questions because he thought he had made his points clearly. When Mills asked Joslyn why he did not understand the text, Joslyn replied that Mills's writing was awkward, unclear, needlessly abstract, and difficult to follow. Somewhat shaken, Mills quickly recovered and unabashedly said, 'I want to become a good writer. I almost have an orgasm when I read a beautiful sentence. Teach me to write.' Joslyn agreed, but thought Mills didn't really mean it. However, Mills persisted and Joslyn tore into the manuscripts. Mills's writing quickly improved. The contrast in writing style between his pre-1943 articles and dissertation and later pieces is striking. (Form, 1995, para. 28).

2. In reviewing *The Power Elite* Robert Bierstedt had this to say about Mills's language:

> A generous admiration for his enterprise, however, must be tempered by a few hesitations. The author's language, for example, is loaded. Members of corporate boards of directors are "commissars," admirals and generals are "warlords," and there is a political "directorate." Mills views the Ivy League and its products with something like a sneer, and for "celebrities" he has little use. He rails against "monstrous decisions" made in an "undemocratically impudent manner," at the "public mindlessness" which permits these proceedings, and at the "organized irresponsibility" it encourages and the "higher immorality" which results. (Bierstedt, 1956, para. 3)

Talcott Parsons about the same book noted,

> Finally, it should be mentioned that in this, as in some of his previous writings, Mills's general tone toward both men and institutions is sharply caustic. *The Power Elite* certainly purports to be an exposition and an explanation of what has been happening in American society, but it is equally an indictment. There is no pretense of even trying to maintain a scientific neutrality; the book is a fiery and sarcastic

attack on the pretensions of the "higher circles" in America either to competence in exercise of their responsibilities or to moral legitimation of their position ... In his combination of often insightful exposition and analysis, empirical one-sidedness and distortion, and moral indictment and sarcasm, Mills reminds one more of Veblen than of any other figure; that he has attained the stature of Veblen I question, but the role he is cutting out for himself is similar (Parsons, 1957, para. 17).

3. Mills added that although the middle-class monopoly on a high school education has been broken, the United States still has not reached a situation of equality of educational opportunity. Far too many are still unable to complete high school because of economic circumstances (1951, p. 267).

4. In the white-collar world, Mills claimed, personality rather than skill is often the more decisive on getting and keeping a job.

5. Mills, it must be noted, was always very clear in stating his values, though perhaps not as successful in avoiding bias.

6. Mark Twain is reputed to have written, "To a man with a hammer everything looks like a nail." Some sources, however, attribute this same quote to Jane Fonda.

7. That there is a true "national interest" other than defense against foreign aggression may well be a myth perpetrated by elites, according to some. Our "national interests" rarely seem to benefit some groups such as the poor, minorities, and women. Howard Zinn (1980) observes that "Nations are not communities and never have been. The history of any country, presented as the history of a family, conceals fierce conflicts of interest (sometimes exploding, more often repressed) between conquerors and the conquered, masters and slaves, capitalists and workers, dominators and dominated in race and sex. And in such a world of conflict, a world of victims and executioners, it is the job of thinking people, as Albert Camus suggested, not to be on the side of the executioners" (p. 10). Interestingly, Howard Zinn, like many of the theorists discussed in this book, has strong connections to Columbia University.

8. Information provided by Mills on his background, or stories about Mills's early life, sexual exploits, and other personal information must be handled with caution. Horowitz has pointed out that Mills often disguised his faults by "admitting to even worse faults" (1983, p. 6). He was a character who delighted in exaggeration and offending others. Indeed, Horowitz reported, most of those who knew him had few good things to say about him personally.

9. There are contradictory characterizations of the relationship between Gerth and Mills. It appears they had several disagreements over credit and control of their joint work. Oakes and Vidich (1999) depict the disputes as bitter and Mills as petty and egotistical. Horowitz (1983), a biographer who recognized many faults of the man, also wrote of the arguments between the two. However, he has attributed much of the problem to Gerth, characterizing him as

being somewhat resentful because his student had eclipsed him. Horowitz also noted that although Gerth clearly did the translations, Mills's hand is readily apparent.

> The primary role of Mills was in editing the editor's work on Weber. In addition, Mills helped to place the extensive introductory essay on Weber within a meaningful American as well as English-speaking context. If the strictly biographical portions of the introduction are clearly written by Gerth, the political analyses and implications are just as clearly the mark of Mills. (Horowitz, 1983, p. 188)

John Summers (2000), a Mills biographer, has attributed Oakes and Vidich's (1999) characterization as an attempt at discrediting Mills rather than being founded on any firm evidence, "placing him [Mills] in the worst possible light at every turn" (para. 14). Instead, Summers characterized the relationship between Gerth and Mills as far more complex and the prevailing standards of publication and credit as far murkier than they are today.

Evidence that Summers and Horowitz are closer to the reality of the Gerth and Mills relationship is contained in several of the letters included in *C. Wright Mills Letters and Autobiographical Writings* (2000). In one letter directly addressing a mix-up in the order of their names for *From Max Weber*, first in a press release from Oxford University Press, and then in a review article that appeared in *Politics*, Mills wrote to his friend.

> Finally, Gerth, let me say flatly to you, in view of the recurrence of the mix-up in the order of our names, that I am most sincerely in full and intimate agreement that you are the senior author in all that we have done with Max Weber, that I am not only content, internally and externally, with being the junior author of the book, but am most grateful to have had the chance to learn what I have of Max Weber while acting as the junior author in collaboration with you. (Mills, 2000, p. 86).

Of course, Mills, who had an interest in conveying an impression, wrote these letters. Mills's daughters, who are concerned with preserving his reputation, also selected the letter for inclusion in the volume. Perhaps more convincing evidence in favor of Summers's characterization of the relationship lies in the fact that Gerth and Mills exchanged letters and visits throughout Mills's life (a seemingly rare feat for any of Mills's friends). Also, Gerth spoke movingly at a memorial service at Columbia for Mills: "He has traversed the course of his life with the tempestuousness of a swift runner. Death struck him down. I have lost my friend, as the Romans used to say, my 'alter ego.' Requiescas in Pace" (Mills, 2000, p. 340).

2

Marvin Harris's
Cultural Materialism

Lacking commitment to any single theory, many social scientists today spin out seemingly endless explanations and mini theories that contribute little understanding to what is going on. Harris was a throwback to the classical theorists in the sense that he was openly committed to a macrotheoretical scheme. Cultural materialism is an ecological-evolutionary systems theory that attempts to account for the origin, maintenance, and change of sociocultural systems.

The foundation of Harris's theory of cultural materialism (CM) is that a society's mode of production (technology and work patterns, especially in regard to food) and mode of reproduction (population level and growth) in interaction with the natural environment has profound effects on sociocultural stability and change. Societies are systems, Harris asserts, and widespread social practices and beliefs must be compatible with the infrastructures of society (the modes of production and reproduction and their interaction with the environment). The infrastructure represents the ways in which a society regulates both the type and amount of resources needed to sustain a society.

A good deal of Harris's work, therefore, is concerned with explaining cultural systems (norms, ideologies, values, beliefs) and widespread social institutions and practices through the use of population, pro-duction, and ecological variables. The infrastructure represents technologies and practices by which sociocultural systems adapt to their environments. Because this activity is so crucial to the survival of individuals and sociocultural systems, Harris maintains, the adoption of these technologies will have tremendous impact on human institutions, cultural values, and beliefs.

Harris fully explored the impact of productive and reproductive factors on social institutions as well as widespread ideals, ideologies, and beliefs. However, contrary to many assertions, Harris did not claim that structural and superstructural factors are merely dependent upon a society's infrastructure. Rather, he saw structural and superstructural factors in interaction with population level and production processes. Society is a system, Harris continually asserted, and while infrastructural practices are primary causal factors in determining the character of that system, structural and superstructural factors play a role as well. The strategy, however, is to fully explore infrastructural-environmental relationships first.

Harris's framework is capable of integrating a diverse range of theoretical insights and empirical observations within its scope. In particular, Harris's concept of structure and superstructure can be further developed to incorporate more diverse sociological and anthropological theory (see Elwell, 1999). But his insistence that relationships between population and production are at the base of all sociocultural systems, and that this base must necessarily have a profound effect on the rest of the system, are the core of Cultural Materialist theory.

Many classical theorists have influenced Marvin Harris, but he is especially beholden to T. Robert Malthus and Karl Marx.[1] From Malthus, Harris borrows his focus on relationships between population and food-production, as well as the effects of population growth on both the environment and the rest of the social system. From Karl Marx, Harris borrows the emphasis on the forces of production as the foundation of social systems.

Ironically, Malthus and Marx are probably the two most maligned and misunderstood of the classical theorists. There is a tendency for critics to mangle and then quickly dismiss their work. (Actually, Marx had a good deal to do with the misrepresentation of Malthus's theory.) It is ironic because Harris's work has also been maligned. However, again like Malthus and Marx, Harris is far more subtle and prescient than his critics give him credit for.

While he did not make up the theoretical perspective from whole cloth, Harris is responsible for the most systematic statements of the cultural materialist research strategy. Through numerous books, chief among them *The Rise of Anthropological Theory* (1968), *Cultural Materialism* (1979), and *Theories of Culture in Postmodern Times* (1999), he has also been the major proselytizer for the perspective. The reaction of anthropologists can be gleaned from the subtitle of the book *Cultural Materialism: The Struggle for a Science of Culture*. The struggle within anthropology much resembles the "paradigmatic revolutions" of Thomas Kuhn (1962), and has become hard-fought on both sides. In *Cultural Materialism* Professor Harris not only systematically presents the research strategy of cultural materialism, but vigorously critiques other competing strategies (and non strategies) in anthropology and sociology. While Harris has gained many adherents within anthropology, cultural materialism remains an embattled perspective that has been attacked vigorously by critics within the discipline (see for example, Adams, 1968; Monaghan, 1986; Beidelman, 1980). In sociology, with the exceptions of Sanderson (1990; 1999; 2005) and Elwell (1992; 1999), the perspective has been largely ignored.

ASSUMPTIONS

Like most macro social theory, cultural materialism is based on the assumption that society is made up of component parts that are functionally interrelated. When one of these component parts changes, other parts must adjust to that change. An institution such as the family cannot be looked at in isolation from other parts of the sociocultural system—from other institutions (say economic, political, or religious) nor from cultural beliefs and ideologies. For example, in order to fully comprehend the recent changes in the American family, the rise in divorce, single-headed households, the decline in family size, and the increase in daycare, you must relate these changes to changes in the economy (say the rising cost of living), as well as changing cultural beliefs (such as the rise of consumerism). When one part of the sociocultural system changes it has effect on many other parts of the system. While viewing society as a system of interrelated parts is at the core of most macro social theory, theories differ in terms of what components are considered to be most important or central in determining the rest of the sociocultural system. Theories also differ on the weight to assign these central components—some going so far as claiming that these central components "completely determine" other parts of the system (various forms of Marxism), others settling more for a strong influence expressed in terms of probabilities.

The second major assumption upon which CM is based is that the foundation of sociocultural systems is the environment. Like all life forms, human beings must take energy from their environment in order to survive. All life, including humans, must therefore live within the constraints of their immediate environment. The two major environmental constraints are the continued availability of natural resources and the tolerance of the environment (including people) for pollution. While human action can modify these constraints—say by devising new technologies to produce more food, or engaging in social practices to limit further population growth—these environmental constraints can never be eliminated or completely overcome. Human technology can never create resources just tap into those resources that exist in nature. Technologies can modify the *type* and *amount* of resources needed for survival, and increases or decreases in human reproduction can modify the *amount* of resources required, but no combination of the two can eliminate our ultimate dependence on the environment. Since our relationships to the environment are essential to human life itself, social practices that serve to modify environmental constraints must have great impact on the rest of the sociocultural system, must be central to understanding any widespread social practice, ideology, or belief in that system.

UNIVERSAL PATTERNS

According to CM, all human societies are patterned along similar lines. Based on the physical environment, all components of sociocultural systems can be organized into:

> Infrastructure
> Structure
> Superstructure

The material infrastructure consists of the technology and social practices by which a society fits into its environment. It is through the infrastructure that a society manipulates its environment by modifying the amount and type of resources needed for the survival of its population. Harris divides the infrastructure into two parts: the *Mode of Production*, and the *Mode of Reproduction*. These components of the infrastructure are attempts to strike a balance between population level and the consumption of energy from a finite environment.

The Mode of Production consists of "(t)he technology and the practices employed for expanding or limiting basic subsistence production, especially the production of food and other forms of energy, given the restrictions and opportunities provided by a specific technology interacting with a specific habitat" (Harris, 1979, p. 52). Within the mode of production Harris includes such variables as the technology of subsistence, work patterns, and technological-environmental relationships. The Mode of Reproduction consists of the technologies and social practices employed for expanding, maintaining or limiting population size. In this category Harris lists such social technologies and practices as mating patterns, medical influence on fertility, natality and mortality, contraception, abortion, infanticide, and the nurturance of infants. The technologies and social practices within the mode of re-production are prime determinants of the population size of a sociocul-tural system.

Like all life on earth, human beings must obtain subsistence from their environment. All human action is therefore necessarily limited by environmental constraints, chiefly the availability of food. The amount of food that a particular environment can provide is limited by natural factors (such as land fertility, the existence of animals with potential to be domesticated, climate, rainfall patterns) and human technologies and social practices (such as the domestication of plants and animals, fertil-izers, irrigation, plow, insecticides). The amount of food that a particu-lar sociocultural system needs is also determined by its population size. It is through modifications of the technologies and practices within the infrastructure (both the modes of production and reproduction) that societies increase or decrease the type and amount of resources re-quired from their environment.

One can see how the infrastructure interacts with the environment by considering a hypothetical hunting and gathering band that, because of the depletion of game species, is experiencing hard times. Assuming the band is rooted by tradition to their forest (or hemmed in by power-ful neighbors) they have only a few options. Within the mode of pro-duction they can intensify their hunting practices by working harder or by using better technology to more efficiently hunt animals, or they can broaden their subsistence base to harvest plants and animals that they previously spurned. Within the mode of reproduction they can reduce their population size immediately through such practices as infanticide or geronticide, or more long-term through changes in mating patterns to better space out births. After making some of these adjustments they will again be existing within their environmental constraints until either a change in the natural environment (say a change in climate), or a change in their subsistence technology (say the adoption of the bow and arrow), or population level (say an increase in births) again upsets the balance. Whatever technologies and practices people employ to adjust to these environmental constraints will necessarily have great effect on other parts of the sociocultural system. All sociocultural sys-tems, not just hunting and gathering societies, must live within their environmental limits. These constraints must necessarily be passed on to other parts of the sociocultural system.

Harris terms the second major component of sociocultural systems as the *Structure*. This component consists of the organized patterns of social life carried out among the members of a society. One of the nec-essary survival functions that each society must fulfill is to maintain orderly and secure relationships among individuals, groups, and neighboring societies. The threat of disorder, Harris asserts, comes primarily from the economic process, which allocates labor and products to individuals and groups. Thus Harris divides the structure of sociocultural systems into two parts: the *Political Economy* and the *Domestic Economy*.

The political economy consists of groups and organizations that perform the functions of regulating exchange, consumption, and reproduction between and within groups and other sociocultural systems. This component consists of such elements as political organizations, military, corporations, division of labor, police, service and welfare organizations, as well as professional and labor organizations. The domestic economy represents the organization of reproduction, production, exchange, and consumption within domestic settings (such as households, camps). This part of the structure consists of family, the domestic division of labor, age and sex roles, and friendship networks.

Given the importance of symbolic processes for human health and happiness, Harris also posits the universal existence of a superstructure. Again, Harris divides this component into two parts: the *Behavioral Superstructure* and the *Mental Superstructure*. The behavioral superstructure includes recreation activities, art, sports, rituals, games, science, folklore, and other aesthetic products. The mental superstructure involves the patterned ways in which the members of a society think, conceptualize, and evaluate their behavior. Harris actually posits that these mental categories run parallel to the universal behavioral components of sociocultural systems. Running parallel to the infrastructure, for example, are such mental components as subsistence lore, magic, religious beliefs, and taboos that serve to justify, encourage, and evaluate productive and reproductive behavior. Similar mental superstructural ideologies, beliefs, and taboos serve to justify, encourage, and evaluate behavior occurring in the domestic and political economies and in the behavioral superstructure as well. However, for the sake of simplicity, Harris designates all of these elements as the "mental superstructure," by which he means: "the conscious and unconscious cognitive goals, categories, rules, plans, values, philosophies, and beliefs about behavior elicited from the participants or inferred by the observer" (Harris, 1979, p. 54).

All sociocultural systems, according to Harris as noted earlier, have these three major components: infrastructure, structure, and superstructure. The major principles of cultural materialism concern the interdependent relationships among these component parts.

THE RESEARCH STRATEGY

Harris advocates a specific strategy for analyzing sociocultural systems. When trying to understand or explain a widespread social practice or belief, he urges, always begin with an examination of infrastructural-environmental relations. He calls this the *principle of infrastructural determinism* (a somewhat unfortunate choice of terminology since Harris explicitly recognizes the probabilistic nature of the relationships). Because of these misunderstandings and misinterpretations, Harris later renames this principle the *primacy of the infrastructure* (Harris, 1998, p. 142). The principle is that the mode of production and reproduction (infrastructure) will "probabilistically determine" (strongly effect) the political and domestic structure, which in turn will probabilistically determine the behavioral and mental superstructure. Harris believes that the primacy of the infrastructure should be the guiding strategy in any analysis of a social phenomenon. In examining any widespread sociocultural practice or belief, look to infrastructural factors first. The rationale behind giving the infrastructure such priority rests upon the fact that it is through infrastructural practices that society adapts to its environment by modifying the amount and type of resources required for life (Harris, 1979, p. 57). It is through the infrastructure that society survives. Since these infrastructural practices are essential for life itself, Harris reasons, all widespread structural and superstructural patterns must be compatible with these practices.[2]

A society's infrastructure is the primary cause of stability and change in its structure, and the structure, in turn, is the primary cause of stability and change in its superstructure. Through the principle of the primacy of the infrastructure, cultural materialism provides a logical set of research priorities for the study of sociocultural life. But while the infrastructure is considered to be of primary importance, the structure and superstructure are not mere reflections of infrastructural processes, but are in interaction with the infrastructure (Harris, 1979, pp. 70–75).

Harris considers societies to be very stable systems. The most likely outcome of any change in the system, whether this change originates in the infrastructure, structure, or superstructure, is resistance in the other sectors of society. This system-maintaining negative feedback is capable of deflecting, dampening, or extinguishing most system changes. The result is either the extinction of the innovation or slight compensatory changes that preserve the fundamental character of the whole system.

But structures and superstructures can provide positive feedback to innovations as well, and when this occurs, change is rapid and fundamental—revolutionary in character. In general, sociocultural change that releases more energy from the environment is likely to be swiftly adapted and to stimulate accommodating change within the structure and superstructure.

INDIVIDUAL BEHAVIOR

In the great debate between materialists and idealists, Harris is firmly in the materialist camp (Harris, 1979. pp. 58–62). To assertions that human values or reason are the foundation of society, Harris counters with the claim that mind is formed by challenges presented by environment, and these challenges will always shape human behavior and thought. For Harris, there is a basic imbalance between our ability to have children and our ability to obtain energy for their survival. This basic imbalance between nature and nurture is expressed in individual lives through cost/benefit decisions regarding sexual behavior, children, work, and standard of living.[3]

According to Harris, mankind is relatively free from biological drives and predispositions. As a species, Harris asserts, we have been selected for our ability to learn most of our social behavior rather than for any specific instinctual behavior. The selection processes responsible for the evolution of sociocultural systems occurs at the individual level according to several "selective principles" operating at that level (Harris, 1979, pp. 62–64). These selective principles are the biopsychological cost/benefit calculus that serves to guide human behavior within a given sociocultural system. It is through these individual cost/benefit decisions that human groups and societies change, it is through these adaptations that Harris is able to explain how infrastructure mediates between culture and nature. Harris enumerates four selective principles:

1. People need to eat and will generally opt for diets that offer more rather than fewer calories and proteins and other nutrients.
2. People cannot be totally inactive, but when confronted with a given task, they prefer to carry it out by expending less rather than more human energy.
3. People are highly sexed and generally find reinforcing pleasure from sexual intercourse—most often from heterosexual intercourse.

4. People need love and affection in order to feel secure and happy, and other things being equal, they will act to increase the love and affection that others give them. (1979, p. 63)

Harris makes several observations that serve to justify his selective principles. First, humans share these bio-psychological preferences with other primates. When confronted with a choice between more rather than fewer calories or expending less rather than more energy, primates all tend to opt for the richer diets or the expenditure of less energy. Thus, the generality of Harris's list of universal needs is virtually assured. Second, the list should be judged not on its inclusiveness but on the adequacies of the theories it helps to generate. The more parsimonious the list of selective principles, the more powerful the theories based upon them (1979, p. 63).

The fact that humans have a biopsychological predisposition to maximize their diets or maximize the love given them does not mean that there are not widespread opposing behaviors and thoughts in many societies. Many Americans, for example, have taken the option of diets that offer more rather than fewer calories and proteins to a high art, and now must opt for fewer calories and proteins to maintain their health (though such denial is a discipline, one that many of us have yet to master). Similarly, many in hyperindustrial[4] societies have opted for expending less energy so often that now we must consciously look for ways of exercising the body (though again, this is a discipline). There are vegetarians in the world, there are those who practice sexual abstinence, there are those who murder their children. Also, just because the selective principles push individuals to maximize the diets, sexual satisfaction, energy conservation, and love they receive does not mean that societies are organized around the attainment of these goals for all. Societies are based on finite environments; some can attain their biological and psychological needs more effectively than others can (Harris, 1979, pp. 63–64). The selective principles that guide individual cost/benefit decisions often lead to social paradoxes, puzzles that cultural materialism is particularly well suited to solve. These puzzles include such phenomena as widespread hunger in societies where cattle roam free; the widespread practice of potlatch in which American Indians of the Northwest systematically produced and then destroyed tremendous amounts of goods; or why women in modern America left the home and sought employment in the outside labor force. In fact, for Harris the solving of such puzzles is a central focus of his anthropology.

ROLE OF ELITES

While the selective principles are universal, the ways in which societies meet individual needs for food, energy conservation, sex, and love, as well as the extent to which these needs are met throughout the population of a society, are highly variable. The entire sociocultural system rests on the cost/benefit calculus individuals use to exploit their environments to meet their biopsychological needs. But it is not the simple calculation of the greatest good for the greatest number of people that accounts for sociocultural change. Many changes are more satisfying to some members of society than to others. Changes that enhance the position of elites are likely to be those that receive positive feedback from structural institutions, positive feedback from the dominant ideologies within the society (Harris, 1979, p. 61). Infrastructural changes that enhance the position of elites are likely to be "amplified and propagated" throughout the system. Changes that hurt elite interests are likely to be resisted.

CM is in agreement with Marx that: "The ideas of the ruling class in each epoch are the ruling ideas." The elite are able to impose direct and indirect economic and political sanctions to get their way. Elites also encourage ideas and ideologies favorable to their position. However, CM does not claim absolute rule by an elite. The amount of power and control exercised by an elite is an empirical question; it varies across societies and through time. One of the first tasks of a Cultural Materialist analysis is to attempt to identify the elite within a sociocultural system, gauge the amount of power that they wield, and uncover their interests, biases, and assumptions when analyzing that society.

INTENSIFICATION

Like all life on earth, human beings must expend energy to obtain energy from their environment. Harris notes that the amounts of energy social systems expend to obtain energy have expanded significantly throughout social evolution. Hunting and gathering bands expended less than 100,000 kilocalories per day to get their sustenance. This energy expenditure increases to about 1 million per day for slash-and-burn farming villages, 25 billion per day for irrigation states (Mesopotamia, Mesoamerica), and over 50 trillion per day for hyperindustrial societies (Harris, 1979, p. 67). This expansion in energy budgets has been accompanied by an increase in both human productivity and population, all of which has had dramatic consequences for the rest of the sociocultural system.

"Anthropologists have long recognized that in broadest perspective cultural evolution has had three main characteristics: escalating energy budgets, increased productivity, and accelerating population growth" (Harris, 1979, p. 67). Harris asserts that there is a direct relationship between increases in productivity and population growth. Increases in production cause population to grow, which then further stimulates greater productivity. This is Malthus's application of the law of supply and demand applied to the relationships between food production and population growth. As the food supply increases, food becomes cheaper, and more children survive (or are allowed to survive). As there are more mouths to feed, food becomes more expensive, thus causing more land to be put under the plow or greater investment in time and energy and technology to increase food production. While Malthus (and Harris) recognized that the relationships among the fertility of people and land are a good deal more complex than this simplified assertion, they insist that there is a recurrent reciprocal relationship between the two.

Recall that, according to Malthus (and Harris), our ability to produce children is always greater than our ability to produce energy for their survival. Because necessary checks to population growth are always present, and because until relatively recent times, these checks tend to be violent toward women, fetuses, and children, sociocultural systems use increases in productivity to allow population to expand. Because of this reciprocal relationship between population and production, over the course of sociocultural evolution, both population and food production have grown (Harris, 1979, p. 68). Periods of increase in food productivity, whether it be because of the application of new technology or the expansion of cultivated land, have been met with expansions of population. Periods of stability in food production, or contraction in productivity, have been marked by the same phenomena in population level. Over the course of sociocultural evolution, however, the long-term tendency has been for both productivity and population to intensify. This intensification, according to CM, has great impact on other parts of the sociocultural system.

HARRIS AND MARX

Harris notes that Marx's concepts of the "forces of production" (basically technology) and the "relations of production" (economic organization) have long been the subject of debate. Are the concepts separable, and if so, which has primacy? The orthodox view, he reports, is that Marx merged the two into the "economic foundation of society" (Harris, 1998, pp. 187–188). Harris, however, disagrees with this interpretation and insists that Marx considered the two as separate forces. More important, Harris's definitions of his concepts of infrastructure and structure make clear that he holds the forces of production (which he terms the mode of production, basically technology and work patterns) and the organization of production separately (Harris, 1979, pp. 64–65). He explicitly holds such patterns as the ownership of production facilities, as well as trade, markets, and systems of distribution, as aspects of structures and superstructures (Harris, 1979, pp. 64–65). In this respect, Harris is very much in the Marxist tradition, though he has added wholly new elements of population into the infrastructure as well as his concerns with infrastructural effects on the environment (Harris, 1998, pp. 187–188).

In sum, it is important to realize that technologies and work patterns (infrastructure) and economic organization such as capitalism, socialism, and feudalism (structure) exert separate, independent effects on one another and on the whole. In contrast to Marx, therefore, Harris presents an explicit mode of production consisting of technology and work patterns that people use to make their living from the environment. But Harris's concept of the mode of production is deceptively simple. The mode of production is in complex interaction with demographic and ecological factors, more intensive production processes lead to demographic growth and change, both of which lead to environmental pressures of depletion and pollution. It was with reference to these interactions that Harris described, first the rise of capitalism itself, and then the subsequent industrial revolution. According to Harris, the frantic search for profit or the expansion of capital is one of the main driving forces in the founding and the intensification of the industrial infrastructure.

But capitalism (as well as other structural and superstructural elements) has also been transformed by industrialization. The small entrepreneur employing local workers using traditional handicraft production has given way to the routine employment of thousands around the globe using ever more sophisticated technology in an ever more detailed division of labor, all to maximize productivity. The individual owner of the shop or the factory has given way to stockholders, boards of director, professional managerial staff, and complex bureaucratic organization. Consequently, there has been significant growth in the concentration and centralization of industry; significant changes in the power and authority of the elites at the top of these massive economic organizations. A further consequence of this centralization and concentration are changes in the relationships between these elites and their technocratic and managerial staffs, changes in the relationships between economic and political elites, and consequently changes in the relationships between government and citizen.

Still, despite this complexity, many critics believe that Harris's emphasis on infrastructure slights the influence of structural and superstructural features. However, it should be noted that Harris does accord social organization and ideology independent status. Ideology, social institutions, and political struggle can "enhance or diminish the probability of systemic changes involving all three sectors" (Harris, 1979, p. 72). And this feedback can be significant. It will be seen both in his analyses of the industrial revolution and of modern American society, that structural and superstructural factors associated with capitalism play a significant role in his theory.[5]

But, Harris goes on to say, ideology and political movements cannot successfully (widespread, in the long run) run counter to the way a society exploits its environment. "Cultural materialism holds that innovations are unlikely to be propagated and amplified if they are functionally incompatible with the existing modes of production and reproduction" (Harris, 1979, p. 73). For example, a social movement today to put women back in the home is not likely to garner widespread commitment or success, no matter the ideology or commitment of the advocates, as long as the "industrial infrastructure holds sway" (Harris, 1979, p. 73).

The effects of our vast numbers and powerful technology (including the technology of reproduction) have made it increasingly obvious that infrastructural factors play a key role in sociocultural stability and change. World population and industrial technology, both infrastructural factors, are now massive. Both are presently growing at an exponential rate. It is a sociocultural system. You can't do *one* thing. This tremendous size as well as its recent exponential growth (or intensification) has had tremendous impact on the environment (depletion and pollution) and has caused tremendous change in human organizations, beliefs, and values. Cultural materialism is a research strategy uniquely suited to exploring both short-term sociocultural stability and change, or the long-term social evolutionary process itself. To illustrate the theory we will first outline Harris's explanation of two social evolutionary milestones—the agricultural and industrial revolutions. We will then turn to some more recent changes in contemporary society, specifically the transformation of the American industrial mode of production to one of hyperindustrialism.[6]

THE DOMESTICATION OF PLANTS AND ANIMALS

All humans lived in hunting and gathering societies from the beginning of the species to recent historical times. This is thought to be some 2 million years. During this time there was some slow technological evolution. Tools and weapons were gradually perfected and human groups gradually moved from scavenging to hunting large animals (Harris, 1977, p. 29).

> In Europe and Asia vast herds of reindeer, mammoth, horses, bison, and wild cattle grazed on lush grasses fed by glacial melt waters. The pursuit of these creatures came to dominate the food quest. Hunters rounded up their prey by setting fires, drove them over cliffs, and dispatched them with an arsenal of stone and bone projectile points, spears, darts, long knives, and bows and arrows. For thousands of years human predators and animal prey remained in ecological balance. (Harris, 1977, p. 29)

As the hunters and gatherers became more efficient, their population numbers gradually rose. The growing population would then put pressure on the societies to develop more efficient and effective hunting and gathering techniques, the discovery of which would often spur further population growth. However, through the application of rigorous techniques of population control—particularly infanticide, body-trauma abortion, and the use of natural birth control—hunting and gathering populations remained in rough balance with their environments.[7]

Then, about 11,000 years ago, within a span of a mere 10,000 years, in several isolated places around the globe, groups began to domesticate plants and then animals to first supplement their hunting and gathering mode of production, and then gradually to replace it. There are two notable characteristics of the transition that are of theoretical interest, Harris points out. First, it occurs in several isolated regions: in the Near East about 10,000 years ago, in the New World between 9,000 and 7,000 years ago, and probably in several additional locations in Southeast Asia and West Africa (Harris, 1971, p. 175). All the evidence indicates that these transitions were made independent of one another, without benefit of cultural contact. The second characteristic of interest is that these independent transitions were made in a brief span of time. Human societies had spent 2 million years exploiting their environments exclusively through hunting and gathering. Two million years of gradually improving their tool kits to be sure, but exploiting the same wild resources. Then, within a span of about 10,000 years, one-half of one percent of the total time spent in hunting and gathering, several societies made a transition to relying primarily on domesticated plants and animals for their subsistence. Any theory of the domestication of plants and animals, Harris points out, must explain why it happened in several isolated societies, and why it happened in such a brief period of time (Harris, 1979, p. 85).

Such constraints on a theory of domestication automatically rule out the great-man-or-woman-with-an-idea theory. Such geniuses would have to appear in several different societies, and it would be only a happy coincidence that they would all be born within that short time frame (Harris, 1979, pp. 85–86). Also, Harris points out, hunters and gatherers are keen observers of their environments; they have intimate knowledge of the local plant and animal life. They engage in practices that increase the yield of wild species of plants, they sometimes keep pets, they appear to know the relationship between seed and plant. It is not lack of knowledge that keeps them from domestication.

Harris insists that to explain the global emergence of domestication within a brief span of time the theory must be one of process, not of historical events. Harris begins his explanation by pointing out that about 13,000 years ago the interglacial period began. This period marks the receding of the glaciers of the last ice age.

> The glaciers that had covered much of the Northern Hemisphere with mile-high sheets of ice began to back away toward Greenland. As the climate became less severe, forests of evergreens and birches invaded the grassy plains which nourished the great herds. The loss of these grazing lands in combination with the toll taken by human predators produced an ecological catastrophe. The wooly mammoth, wooly rhinoceros, steppe bison, giant elk, European wild ass, and a whole genus of goats suddenly became extinct. While horses and cattle survived, their numbers in Europe sharply decreased. Other species like the saiga antelope and the musk ox survived only in scattered pockets in the far north. Scientists do not agree about the relative impact of the climatological changes and human predation in bringing about the extinction of these animals. Human predation definitely played a role because elephants and rhinos managed to survive several earlier warming trends caused by previous glacial retreats. (1977, pp. 29–30)

After a slow buildup of population levels over millennia, hunters and gatherers throughout the world confronted a gradually depleting environment. In many areas the first response was to intensify their mode of production, to develop more efficient hunting technologies and practices. These practices were successful for a time but would only speed up the depletion process in the long term (Harris, 1977, pp. 31–37).

The world-wide scale of this event accounts for the simultaneous emergence of domestication in several regions around the globe, the different impact that the receding of the glaciers would have in different ecosystems account for the diversity of agricultural systems that emerged (Harris, 1977, p. 38; 1979, pp. 86-87). It is the different ecosystems that account for the differences between Old and New World agriculture, differences that have severe consequences for all of human history.[8]

In the Old World the domestication of plants and animals occurs simultaneously. In the Middle East, where agriculture first appears, there were both rich grains like wheat, barley, and peas that were suitable for cultivation and potential animals to domesticate such as sheep, goats, pigs, and cattle (Harris, 1977, pp. 38–39). Not only did the cultivation of plants serve to directly feed the population, but they could also feed newly domesticated animals to supply meat. Consequently, Middle East agriculture early on consists of a complete production system, a system that allowed permanent settlements, and very quickly stimulated both population and technological growth.[9]

The New World, in contrast, had wild plants that were much less suitable for domestication and no potential animal domesticates to compare to the cattle, horses, sheep, and goats of the Old World.[10] Consequently, in order to continue getting animal proteins, New World peoples continued to hunt, thus delaying permanent settlements for thousands of years (Harris, 1977, p. 38). During this time New World peoples would continually intensify their hunting, developing more efficient weapons and techniques, all temporarily successful but speeding up the depletion process in the long-run (Harris, 1977, p. 34).[11] Over the course of hundreds of generations, peoples in the highlands of Mexico gradually shifted their subsistence away from hunting and toward their domesticated plants. The intensification of farming led to greater food production, which then led to population growth and the impetus for further intensification of agriculture (1977, pp. 34–35).

It was primarily lack of suitable domesticates that led to the very different levels of development of the Old and the New Worlds. Because of the animal extinctions in the New World at the end of the last Ice Age, there were nothing like sheep, goats, pigs, cattle, or horses that survived to be domesticated; certainly there were no potential domesticates in the highlands of Mexico, where maize originates (Harris, 1989, pp. 488–489). "It set the two hemispheres on divergent trajectories and imparted to each a different pace of development. This explains why it was that Columbus 'discovered' America and Powhatan did not 'discover' Europe, that Cortes conquered Moctezuma rather than the other way around" (Harris, 1977, p. 42).

THE INDUSTRIAL REVOLUTION

In his analysis of the causes of the industrial revolution Harris makes clear that he is not a simple infrastructural determinist. There are two primary causes of the revolution, Harris says, infrastructural intensification which led to depletion of resources in Western Europe, and the economic organization and ideology of capitalism. According to Harris, capitalism is a form of economic *organization*, and as such, belongs in the structure of Harris's universal scheme. It is an amazingly productive economic system, leading to unprecedented increases in food, manufacturing, and the provision of services. It is a great "intensifier," a stimulus to people and organizations to increase their efforts in all manner of productive activities. Even before the industrial revolution, capitalism freed people from traditional restraints, as well as stimulating their ambitions to accumulate wealth (Harris, 1971, p. 265).

Capitalism first develops in Europe between the fourteenth and sixteenth centuries. It is an economic system that represents a radical break from the past. Harris (1999, p. 164) characterizes the distinctive features of capitalism:

> All potentially profitable goods and services brought into market relations to be bought and sold. This includes land, and labor. Harris, after Marx, calls this the "commodification" process.
> The pursuit of profit by individuals and groups in all areas of the distribution and production of goods and services.
> The reinvestment of profits (or capital) in enterprises in order to make more capital.
> Government action in the enforcement of economic contracts, and in allowing the accumulation of capital (without confiscating all profits).

Harris thus makes clear in this initial definition of capitalism that he sees it as an economic system promoting unprecedented intensification of production (Harris, 1977, p. 265). While he believes the rise of capitalism is rooted in the infrastructure (intensification, depletion, demography, and a decentralized agrarian mode of production), the structural and ideological aspects of capitalism provide feedback for further intensification of the mode of production. Capitalism, Harris points out, is a system committed to perpetual growth in production in the name of profit. However, he continues, no system can grow forever. All economic systems are bound by environmental constraints (Harris, 1977, p. 265). It is in the attempts of capitalists to overcome environmental constraints of depletion that the Industrial Revolution is born.[12]

Between 1650 and 1750 Western Europe faced a growing energy crisis. Wood, the primary natural resource in an agrarian society, was becoming scarce. Much of the forests had been cleared to expand the fields and increase agricultural output. Wood was increasingly used in the growing iron, glass, and ship building industries. In the home, it was used not only for energy but also as the primary raw material for making household utensils, wagons, looms, and other tools. Shortages of wood created severe problems that threatened a whole way of life. The crisis became especially acute in England, which was rapidly denuding its forests in the sixteenth and seventeenth century. It was about this time that the English began substituting coal for wood. By 1700 in England, coal was rapidly replacing wood as the primary energy source for both domestic and commercial use. The mining of coal had to be intensified.

Coal was increasingly needed on a massive scale. As coal mines had to be sunk deeper, they would go beneath the water table; water seeped into the shafts. This problem became so severe that some mines had to be abandoned. Early in the eighteenth century, Thomas Savery and Thomas Newcome invented the "atmospheric engine" to pump the water out of the shafts. This engine laid the foundation for James Watt's invention of the first true steam engine later in the century. The steam engine was then quickly adapted to ventilate the mines, lift the coal out of the shafts, and transport the coal to markets. Each technological development called for the development of further technology. In order to exploit reserves of coal more intensively, technology was developed to pump the water out of mines. The steam engine (which converts the new energy source, coal, into mechanical energy), as well as the raw energy of the coal itself, was then used to intensify production in a host of other industries (Harris, 1977, p. 272–273).

In Harris's analysis, then, there are two primary causal factors for the revolution in technology. The first is infrastructural. Intensification of production and resulting population growth led to environmental depletions. England was forced to change its resource base from wood to coal, which led to the technological innovations that made the transition possible. The second reason for the transition, Harris asserts, is capitalism. Capitalism, with its relentless drive for profit, stimulates an unprecedented intensification of productive forces. It does this by stimulating and unleashing the desire for wealth in thousands, orienting their behavior toward both innovation and accumulation. While Harris begins all analysis with infrastructure/environmental relationships, he recognizes that it is a sociocultural *system*. Contrary to many of his critics, he does not reduce all sociocultural practices to mere reflections of infrastructural processes.

HYPERINDUSTRIALISM

Hyperindustrialism is Harris's term for an economy in which the number employed in the production of services-and-information has become greater than the number employed in the production of goods. It is an economy in which the private sector is dominated by huge oligopolies, corporations that are unresponsive to the market and that act much like monopolies in setting price and quality standards. It is big government that runs huge budget deficits in order to provide both relief for the underclass and employment for a large sector of the middle class. It is a workforce that is increasingly fractured by an ever more detailed division of labor, whereby the bulk of the workforce becomes "de-skilled" and more vulnerable to automation. It is a society in which, despite the ever-increasing application of technology, the price of goods and services increases and their quality declines. Hyperindustrialism is, in short, *America Now*.[13] In this book Harris addresses a series of questions. "Why nothing works." "Why the dollar shrank." "Why women left the home." "Why America changed." In answering these questions Harris returns again and again to the theme of the interconnectedness of the component parts of sociocultural systems. By showing these connections he hopes to encourage us to take the first steps in recovering the American dream (Harris, 1981, p. 15).

Bureaucracy plays a central role in Harris's analysis of contemporary American society. Growing size of corporations and governments, centralization of power and authority, and oligopoly in industry are all identified as prime movers in the transformation of America in the last half of the twentieth century. Harris believes that the cause of corporate growth can be identified in one word: capitalism. Under a system of free enterprise, some corporations succeed while others fail. Over time, unless government takes action to counter the tendency, the competitive process produces a few winners that grow to tremendous size

(1981, pp. 25–26 & pp. 166–167). This is, of course, very much in line with Karl Marx. In American society there was an attempt to stop this concentration at the turn of the last century with the passage of antimonopoly laws, but these laws did not stop the formation of oligopolies, which act similarly to stifle competition (1981, pp. 25–26).

Government has expanded in size and scope, Harris argues, in an effort to offset the booms and busts of a capitalist economy (1981, p. 167). Beginning with the Great Depression, the government began following the theories of economist John Maynard Keynes. "Downturns in the cycle were to be controlled by increasing the money supply, by lowering interest rates, and by increasing the level of government expenditures, in various combinations as needed. Once business started to pick up again, these measures were to be reversed" (1981, pp. 61–62). The problem was that while it was relatively easy to increase government spending, it became politically impossible to significantly reduce it when the economy righted itself. Add the gradual decline of the manufacturing as a significant source of employment due to automation, and the government became trapped in a role of massive spending to stimulate the economy as well as a direct and indirect source of jobs (1981, p. 62).[14] In this connection, Harris cites the federal government's failure to balance its budget nineteen out of twenty times between 1960 and 1980, and the consequent pileup of debt of $435 billion (Harris, 1981, p. 64). (The estimated budget deficit for fiscal year 2003–2004 alone is for over $400 billion.)

Perhaps the most widely hailed change experienced by American society since World War II has been the transformation of the economy from goods production to the production of service and information. While many have interpreted this shift as a move toward a "postindustrial" society, Harris is skeptical that it represents such a qualitative change (Harris, 1981, p. 46). While postindustrial enthusiasts call forth images of legions of service workers who consult with corporate leaders, or information workers who analyze the latest trends in consumer behavior, the reality is far different. Most of the jobs created in the service and information economy bear close resemblance to Adam Smith's description of the detail workers in the pin factory (Harris, 1981, pp. 46–47). These are not "postindustrial" jobs that are being created, they are industrial service and information jobs—they rely on essentially unskilled or semi-skilled labor; they are broken down into simple, easily learned steps; and they are poorly paid.

Why are such jobs coming to dominate the American economy? Harris first asserts that because of automation in goods production, a great pool of unskilled and unorganized labor gradually becomes avail-

able. Driven by the spur of profit, businesses and individuals are always looking to invest capital in enterprises that promise a significant
return on investment. The growing size and therefore relative cheap-
ness of the unskilled labor pool encouraged private business to expand
investment in the production of services and information processing
(1981, p. 168). As long as such labor remains cheap and plentiful, there
will be little incentive for companies to invest in technology to replace
such workers. A second factor behind the growth in service and information jobs is the growth of government services and bureaucracy.

Oligopoly, uncontrolled government spending, and an economy
increasingly engaged in the production of services and information
have all combined to shrink the buying power of the U.S. dollar.

> After three decades of the most astonishing labor-saving technologi-
> cal advances in the history of the human species, everything became
> more expensive. Why? Because at the same time that factory automa-
> tion was saving labor and raising productivity, something else was
> wasting labor and lowering productivity on an even grander scale. It
> seems to me that this something else was none other than the rise of
> public and private bureaucratic oligopolies and the shift from a pre-
> dominantly blue-collar to a predominantly pink- and white-collar la-
> bor force. People who work in and for bureaucracies whether at
> white-collar, pink-collar, or blue-collar jobs, become inflexible,
> bored, and alienated. They may turn out more products, information,
> or services per unit-time, but the quality of what they produce suffers.
> And so let us face up to an unpleasant truth: By lowering quality, in-
> dustrial bureaucracy can waste labor as fast as industrial machinery
> can save it. (1981, pp. 168–169)

In a futile effort to maintain living standards, women sought work in
the outside labor force where they were met with open arms by expanding bureaucracies and service agencies. The integration of women into
the paid labor force, particularly married women, contributed mightily
to changes in family structure. In short, the transition fundamentally
changes the entire society.

EXCURSUS: RECENT INTENSIFICATION OF THE AMERICAN INFRASTRUCTURE

In this section we will briefly examine the growth of the infrastructure
in American society over the last twenty years or so, and sketch out
some of the ways these changes have affected the rest of the sociocul-

tural system. One way to describe the character and size of productive activities within a nation state is through the Gross Domestic Product or GDP. GDP is the broadest measure of the productivity (or "health") of an economy. It is defined as the market value of goods and services produced within a country. Table 2.1 displays the US GDP for selected years from 1987 to 2001. In 1987, the Gross Domestic Product of the United States was $4.7 trillion. In 2001 the GDP stood at slightly over $10 trillion. This represents more than a doubling in the size of GDP in just thirteen years, an increase of over $5 trillion (both measures are in 2001 dollars, inflation therefore is not a factor).

The mode of production in hyperindustrial societies grows exponentially. The annual growth rate of the GDP for American society has averaged around 4 to 6 percent for years. But the distinguishing characteristic of hyperindustrial society is not the exponential growth rate. Such growth rates are characteristic of industrial societies as well. What is really novel about hyperindustrial society is the level of its economic base. Exponential growth applied to an economy already this massive produces tremendous real growth.[15] It took over 100 years of increasingly intensive industrialization to achieve a GDP of just under $5 trillion. It took only an additional fourteen years of further intensification to achieve the next $5 trillion. If, as Harris claims, the mode of production is one of the primary factors behind change in sociocultural systems, then this growth should be causing considerable turmoil in other parts of the sociocultural system. As we will see, it is.[16]

Table 2.1 also displays the percent of GDP accounted for by private and government industries, as well as a breakdown by industry type. As can be seen, private industry has grown from producing 86 percent of all the goods and services in the nation, to 87 percent. This is not an insignificant gain when talking an economy of $10 trillion. Government at all levels—local, state, and federal—is the mirror image of this, losing almost 1 percent of GDP over the fourteen-year span. This is perhaps due to all of the "privatization" initiatives taken during the time period in schools, prisons, medicine, and other government services.

Also displayed in the table are two industries that have gained significantly: "Finance, insurance, and real estate," and "Services." The first category is self-explanatory: The big items within this group include depository institutions (banks and savings and loans), real estate companies, insurance carriers, and security and commodities brokers. The service category includes personal services, auto repair and services, motion pictures, health, and education.

Table 2.1: GDP by Industry for Selected Years 1987-2001

	1987	1990	1994	1998	2001
Gross Domestic Product (in millions of current dollars)	4,742,462	5,803,246	7,054,315	8,781,527	10,062,151
Private Industry (Percent GDP)	86.1	86.1	86.4	87.4	87.3
Agriculture, forestry, and fishing	1.9	1.9	1.7	1.5	1.4
Mining	1.9	1.9	1.3	1.1	1.4
Construction	4.6	4.3	3.9	4.3	4.8
Manufacturing	18.7	17.9	17.3	16.3	14.1
Transportation and public utilities	9.0	8.5	8.7	8.3	8.1
Wholesale trade	6.5	6.5	6.8	6.9	6.8
Retail trade	9.2	8.9	8.8	9.0	9.2
Finance, insurance, and real estate	17.5	17.4	17.8	19.5	20.6
Services	16.7	18.5	19.4	20.8	22.1
Government (Percent GDP)	13.9	13.9	13.6	12.6	12.7

Source: Bureau of Economic Analysis, U.S. Department of Commerce.

The big loser, in relative terms, is manufacturing, going from 18.7 percent of GDP to 14.1 percent in 2001. However, it is too soon to be writing of the demise of American manufacturing. While this sector has lost in terms of the percent of GDP in the United States, it has actually grown in real dollar terms, going from $888,592,000,000 in 1987 to $1,422,990,000,000 in 2001, a gain of 60 percent. Manufacturing is a smaller percentage of GDP in 2001 because GDP more than doubled in size in the same time period.[17] Manufacturing, both in terms of product and employment, remains an integral part of hyperindustrial economy.[18] The term "hyperindustrial" recognizes that the economy is dynamic and changing—services, information and finance are an increasingly important part of the economy. However, there are limits to this development; an agricultural, mining, and manufacturing base are all also essential components of a hyperindustrial economy.

Population is the second infrastructural factor that Harris posits will have profound effects on the rest of the sociocultural system. Table 2.2 displays the population history of the United States for each census year from 1790 to 2000. It also displays the actual numerical increase for each period, the rate of the increase for each decade, the percent of the population that is urban, and the density or the number of people per square mile. Several interesting facts are displayed in the table. First, note that although the actual rate of increase is quite large in the period from 1790 to 1870, the numerical increase in population for each decade remains in single digits (in millions). The rate of increase actually peaks with the initial wave of industrialization during the 1850s and 60s, though the numerical increase begins to grow rapidly shortly after. Since the 1860s the rate of increase has declined dramatically, from the peak of 35.9 percent, down to the last completed decade of 1990 to 2000 of only 13.2 percent. But note the actual numerical increase for this same time period.

Like the economy (or the lily), the population level is quite substantial by 1880. Ever smaller growth rates produce ever larger effects. For example, despite the fact that the rate of increase from 1990 to 2000 was only 13.2 percent, the actual numerical increase in population for that decade (32,712,033 people added) was greater than the total population level of the United States in 1860 (31,443,321). These 32 million additional people in the 1990s all have to be housed, clothed, fed, socialized, loved, policed, and provided a variety of services. Again, it is not exponential growth of population that distinguishes hyperindustrial society; it is the rapidity of real physical growth.

There are three factors that determine population level: fertility, mortality, and migration. As a nation, U.S. fertility has declined with industrialization. Part of the decline in fertility is due to a postponement of marriage and children as young women attend college or enter the workforce and young couples take time to establish themselves economically. The median age at first birth for U.S. women has climbed from 21.8 years in 1960 (the tail end of the baby boom) to 24.5 years in 1999 (Kent and Mather, 2002, pp. 6–7). This means such women have fewer years to have children once they start. A second reason behind the declining fertility rate is the ready availability of contraceptives, making it easier for women to control their fertility.

While fertility rates have declined in the United States since the 1960s, they are somewhat higher than the fertility rates of other industrial societies. The average fertility rate of more developed countries is 1.6 children born per woman, which is below replacement level. In the United States in 2002, the fertility rate was 2.1 (Kent and Mather, 2002, p. 8). One reason why the fertility rate in the U.S. is somewhat higher than other industrial nations might be that the United States makes it easier than other nations for women to combine work and family. Such factors as higher employment rates in the United States, more affordable housing and other commodities may make slightly larger families more affordable (Kent and Mather, 2002, p. 8).

Table 2.2: U.S. Population, 1790–2000

Census Year	Total Population	Increase	Increase %	Urban %	Density (Persons per sq. mi.)
1790	3,929,214	-	-	5.1	4.5
1800	5,308,483	1,379,269	35.1	6.1	6.1
1810	7,239,881	1,931,398	36.4	15.4	4.3
1820	9,638,453	2,398,572	33.1	7.2	5.5
1830	12,860,702	3,222,249	33.4	8.8	7.4
1840	17,063,353	4,202,651	32.7	10.8	9.8
1850	23,191,876	6,128,523	35.9	15.4	7.9
1860	31,443,321	8,251,445	35.6	19.8	10.6
1870	38,558,371	7,115,050	22.6	25.7	10.9
1880	50,189,209	11,630,838	30.2	28.2	14.2
1890	62,979,766	12,790,557	25.5	35.1	17.8
1900	76,212,168	13,232,402	21.0	39.6	21.5
1910	92,228,496	16,016,328	21.0	45.6	26.0
1920	106,021,537	13,793,041	15.0	51.2	29.9
1930	123,202,624	17,181,087	16.2	56.1	34.7
1940	132,164,569	18,961,945	15.4	56.5	37.2
1950	151,325,798	19,161,229	14.5	64.0	42.6
1960	179,323,175	27,997,377	18.5	69.9	50.6
1970	203,302,031	23,978,856	13.4	73.6	57.5
1980	226,542,199	23,240,168	11.4	73.7	64.0
1990	248,709,873	22,167,674	9.8	75.2	70.3
2000	281,421,906	32,712,033	13.2	81.0	79.6

Source: U-S-history.com, accessed 6/3/2004 at http://www.u-s-history.com/pages/h980.html

A large part of the reason for the higher U.S. rate is that minorities have a somewhat higher fertility rate. While racial and ethnic minorities account for 31 percent of the population, they accounted for 42 percent of the births in 2001 (Kent and Mather, 2002, p. 10). Kent and Mather attribute the difference in fertility to lower educational attainment for most minorities, and recent immigration on the part of Hispanics.

Much of U.S. population growth, at least since the 1980s, has been fueled by legal and illegal immigration. "Between July 1, 2000 and July 1, 2001, the U.S. population grew by nearly 2.7 million people: 1.6 million from the excess of births over deaths, and 1.1 million from net international migration.... Natural increase accounted for about 60 percent of the growth, while net international migration contributed nearly 40 percent" (Kent and Mather, 2002, p. 6). Gauging the contribution of immigration to U.S. population growth by just looking at net migration is probably misleading. Immigrants tend to be in their prime child bearing years. They come to the United States to seek work and to establish a family. Many, particularly Hispanics, come from countries where families tend to be larger (Kent and Mather, 2002, p. 10). As a result, immigrants contribute to population growth through their fertility as well, about one in five babies born in the United States in 2000 was to a foreign born mother (Kent and Mather, p. 19).

More immigrants are attracted to the U.S. than to any other nation. Why such a high rate of immigration? A major part of the pull to the United States lies in perceived economic opportunity. Population level and rate of growth, of course, are intimately related to economic growth. Population growth means more available workers, more consumers, and thus a growing Gross Domestic Product. In fact, it is estimated that population growth alone accounts for over half of all recent economic growth in the United States[19] (Miller, 2004, p. 202). Not only does population growth account for a significant part of the growth in Gross National Product, but for GNP per capita as well.

Another reason for the high level of immigration in the United States is the fairly liberal immigration laws, at least compared to many other industrial nations. There are many reasons for these liberal immigration laws. Founded as the United States was by immigrant groups, there is some national pride in the value and tradition of being a society open to the politically and economically repressed—though this is tempered by our distrust of foreigners as well as certain racial and ethnic prejudices. A second factor behind our liberal immigration laws lies in the interests of businesses that have an interest in encouraging skilled professions as well as adding to the general labor pool. Finally, there are other groups that have an interest in liberal immigration laws, such as the Democratic Party that often gets the vote when immigrants become citizens, recently naturalized citizens who want to allow their family and compatriots access, and the wealthy who have a need for servants and nannies. In addition, because of geography (including a southern border with few natural barriers) and closeness to Latin America, as well as all of the interest groups listed above, the United States has a high amount of illegal immigration as well.

Both legal and illegal immigration fluctuates with political and economic conditions. While the United States has a political history of openness to immigration, there is also an undercurrent of nativism. High economic growth rates and the success of businesses and others lobbying governments to liberalize immigration of both types can lead to increases in immigration. Political oppression or poor economic conditions in the rest of the world (particularly in Latin America) also increase the immigration rates.

Immigration affects the ethnic and racial makeup of a population.

> Social scientists have studied the effects of immigration on wages, tax revenues, government expenditures, and other social and economic features of American life and have come to varying and sometimes contradictory conclusions. Some see the current immigrants as adding to the public burden by using more public services than they pay for in taxes. Immigrants, for example, burden public schools with non-English-speaking children, hold down wages for U.S.-born residents, and add to the costs of public health and other services. Others argue that the benefits of immigration outweigh the burdens: They point out that, for example, immigrants take jobs others do not want, pay taxes, and inject vitality and richness into American society. (Kent and Mather, 2002, pp. 24–25)

Population growth—net fertility and immigration—also affects the age and sex structure of the population. The age and sex structure of the United States in 1900 was pyramidlike, with a large youthful population at the base and each succeeding cohort being a little smaller, leading to a small elderly population at the top of the pyramid. Because of changing mortality, fertility, and immigration rates throughout the century this pyramid has become somewhat distorted, with a bulge of baby boomers now in late middle age near the top of the pyramid, slightly smaller cohorts just under this group (the baby bust), but fairly substantial younger cohorts. Because both fertility and immigration are higher in the United States than other developed countries, it has a much younger base than other industrial countries.

The age and sex structure of a population affects life chances as well as future population and economic growth. Kent and Mather (2002) summarize one cohort theory:

> The relative size of a cohort is important because it determines the number of people who are competing for the same jobs, promotions, federal entitlements, and other limited resources. Economist Richard Easterlin theorized that people born into a cohort that is smaller than the preceding one would encounter less competition for jobs and earn higher incomes, which would encourage them to marry earlier and have more children. This might explain why Americans born in the 1930s, when fertility was relatively low, produced the baby boom by marrying and starting families at younger ages than their parents or even their older siblings. People born into a cohort that is substantially larger than the preceding one would encounter more job competition and lower relative wages, causing them to delay marriage and childbearing. The relative cohort theory might explain the baby boomers' marked postponement of marriage and childbearing, which led to plummeting fertility rates in the mid-1970s. (p. 27) [20]

Because the United States has a much younger age profile than other industrial nations it will continue to grow, particularly if fertility rates remain stable and immigration continues at its present levels. And this will lead to economic growth. But the age and sex structure of a population is not simply related to population and economic growth; it often has impact upon social structures as well.

One example of how the age and sex structure affects other parts of the sociocultural system is found in the general aging of the American population. First begun with the industrial revolution and the decline of infant mortality, the aging of the population has had a dramatic effect on United States government and politics. The 1930s saw the passage of the Social Security Act specifically designed to entice many older workers out of the workforce. The creation of Medicare in the 1960s and the focus of the Welfare State on the income and medical needs of the elderly since that time can be directly attributed to their growing numbers as well as their high voting participation rates.

Another well-known example is the baby boom phenomenon in the United States that occurred from 1947 through about 1963. The baby boom has often been likened to a "pig in a python." Each year from 1947 through 1957 an additional 1 million babies were born than the previous year. As the huge age cohort advanced through first elementary schools, then secondary schools, and then colleges, it caused tremendous growth and disruption. The cohort became the center of attention of the culture, the focus of the market place. In college the cohort burst the seams, engaging in massive protests against the war in Vietnam, against the university, and against the political and economic system. Pouring out of the colleges beginning in the early 1970s, the cohort faced increasingly stiff competition in the job market. As stated above, this competition forced them to delay marriage and children. As the cohort ages, the market place continues to pander to its wants and needs—yuppies, exercise, dieting, Viagra. As the cohort begins to reach retirement age (beginning in about 2010) it will place a tremendous strain on the social security system.[21]

Two final population characteristics of note about hyperindustrial America are that (1) growth rates are uneven around the country due to internal and international migration and uneven economic development; and that (2) population density is rising and the country is becoming more urban. Economic development often attracts domestic and international migration. Migrants tend to be young and have interest in establishing families. This population growth, of course, stimulates further economic growth. States in the south and the west are growing faster than midwestern and northern states (Kent and Mather, 2002, p. 33), the fastest growing include California, Texas, and Florida. Other states are experiencing much slower growth or even population decline. Table 2.2 also displays the increasing urbanization and density within the country. About 80 percent of the U.S. population in 2000 lives in urban areas, twice the percentage than at the end of the last century. Density has almost doubled between 1950 and 2000 going from 43 to about 80 people per square mile.

Such is a quick sketch of the infrastructure—the mode of production and population—of American hyperindustrial society. According to Harris (echoing others), both production and population are key components of the sociocultural system; they are the way a society fits into its environment, the way a society ensures its own survival. Any widespread institutional structures (say, family, educational system, or government) and values and ideologies (Christianity, liberalism) must be consistent with this infrastructure, must be compatible with the way people go about exploiting their environment to make a living. As systems theorists (and ecologists) are fond of telling us, you can't do *one* thing. Both economic intensification and population growth are interrelated and have independent and combined effects on the rest of the sociocultural system. Economic growth per capita has manifest and latent functions of promoting the arts, producing entertainments, and providing comforts for many individuals and for society as a whole. It is through economic growth that we have funded advances in science, spread education and literacy, and enabled many to partake in the good life. Population growth has led not only to economic growth but also to technological development, the diversity of our culture, and our increasingly urban lifestyle.

But what are the dysfunctions of infrastructural intensification? An extensive examination of the dysfunctions of population and economic intensification would include the following hypotheses:

> Growth in population and production are based on a finite environment. There are limits to the amount of depletion and pollution that can be tolerated by the natural environment. While the emphasis on GDP expansion in the U.S. is gradually shifting away from manufactured goods and toward financial and service categories, the base of all economic activity is still (and must necessarily remain) resource extraction, agriculture, and the production of physical goods.

> The growth and the creative destruction of industry as well as the growth and decline of population create disruption in the life of the community. Uneven growth is especially disruptive. Communities must expand and contract employment, schools, water and sewer lines, roads, and other community facilities to respond to the changes brought about by such a dynamic infrastructure.

> The need for individual and family mobility because of the ever changing needs of the economy have personal costs as well. Such transients are unlikely to put down deep roots, unlikely to join civic organizations, make neighborhood ties, or identify closely with place. Geographical mobility has placed great stress on extended families. With dual career families becoming increasingly common, it is creating increasing stress on nuclear families as well.

> The overall expansion of the economy and growth in population are among the primary causes of the growth and centralization of public and private bureaucracy. This has put inordinate economic, political, and social power and authority into the hands of a few at the top of these organizations. This shift in power and authority was first identified by Mills and has become even more pronounced since his time.

> The expansion of industrial capitalism has led to the commodification of social life. More and more of the goods and services that used to be supplied by family or communities are increasingly being integrated into the market economy (or the "big bazaar" of Mills). The pervasive

exposure to advertising has created a consumer culture based on comfort, consumption, and instant gratification.

Another consequence of the economic expansion is the turmoil created in the U.S. occupational structure. The constant churning of the economy has meant the disruption of lives through unemployment, the loss of skills by many, and the growing dependence of the middle class on corporate and bureaucratic organization for their livelihood.[22]

All of these structural changes—disruption of community, growth in bureaucracy, commodification, and changes in occupational structure (particularly the detailed division of labor)—have contributed to the rationalization of social life.

A final dysfunction of the incredible economic expansion and growing population is a widening inequality both within the nation as well as between nations.

Harris's "primacy of the infrastructure" in explaining sociocultural stability and change is a very viable research strategy.

ABOUT HARRIS

Marvin Harris was born on August 18, 1927 in Brooklyn, New York. He grew up in Brooklyn and attended Erasmus High School. He then entered Columbia College, served in the U.S. Army Air Forces from 1945 to 1947, and graduated with an A.B. from Columbia in 1949. It was as an undergraduate that he took a two-semester anthropology course taught by Charles Wagley. It was in Wagley's course, he reports, where he became "intrigued by a discipline that called for more field trips than office work" (Harris, 1977, "About the Author"). Wagley served as his mentor, invited him on a field trip to South America, and eventually convinced him to attend graduate school at Columbia. Wagley, who was to become his dissertation advisor, also became a collaborator on several books and articles. Harris received his Ph.D. from Columbia in 1953, his thesis a study of rural life in Brazil. Upon graduation, he became an assistant professor at Columbia in 1953, an associate in 1959, and a full professor beginning in 1963. From 1963 to 1966 he chaired the anthropology department at Columbia.

By several accounts Harris was an excellent teacher, his critical style going over well with students in his theory classes at Columbia and later at Florida (Margolis and Kottak, 2003, p. 688; Burns, 2001). His major work, *The Rise of Anthropological Theory* (affectionately known as the RAT) was a product of a graduate course in theory Harris gave while at Columbia in the 1960s. "The course critiqued what he saw as prevailing idealist and idiographic approaches in anthropology. The continued dominance of such paradigms, in what he viewed as their various transformations (ethnoscience, symbolic and interpretive anthropology, structuralism, and postmodernism) would concern him until his death" (Margolis and Kottak, 2003, p. 688). It was in the RAT that Harris first introduced his materialistic research strategy for explaining sociocultural stability and change.

Like others of his generation, Harris was well trained in four-field anthropology—physical anthropology, archaeology, cultural anthropology, and linguistics (Margolis & Kottak, 2003, p. 685). Harris served as president of the General Anthropology Division (GAD) of the American Anthropological Association (AAA) from 1998 to 1990. "Concerned about the fragmentation and compartmentalization of anthropology, he and his successors established the GAD as the strongest voice of four-field anthropology within the AAA" (Margolis and Kottak, 2003, p. 688).

Over the course of his career Harris wrote for several different audiences. Like most social scientists he began his career writing professional articles for colleagues. He then moved to texts for graduates and then for undergraduates. He was successful in each of these endeavors. Both his undergraduate text *Culture, People, Nature: An Introduction to General Anthropology,* which is in the four-field tradition, and *Cultural Anthropology* with Orna Johnson have been through numerous editions. Beginning with *Cannibals and Kings* (1977) Harris attempted to reach a broader, more general audience. Like Mills before him, he felt strongly that social scientists had an obligation to reach this broader audience, had an obligation to reassert the importance of rational thought and objective analysis as a first step in truly governing ourselves and attempting to establish a more just and equitable society.

NOTES

1. Of all the contemporary theorists dealt with in this volume, Harris is perhaps the most thoroughly grounded in classical theory. One of the works early in his career was *The Rise of Anthropological Theory* (affectionately known as RAT among many graduate students) considered a classic and still widely used in the field.

2. Harris, of course, did not simply make up this principle but bases it on the insights of social theorists and observations of social scientists in the past. The principle of infrastructural determinism is specifically based on a reformulation of the insights of Karl Marx (production) and T. Robert Malthus (reproduction). Harris's unique contribution is in clearly defining both population and production variables (eliminating the obscuring "dialectic" from Marx and the moral angst from Malthus) and in combining and interrelating these two powerful forces in the infrastructure.

3. This is very much influenced by Malthus.

4. The prefix "hyper" denotes "over and above," even to the point of "abnormal excess." To describe contemporary America as "hyperindustrial" is to stress both its continuity with the past and how it is rapidly changing even to abnormal excess. This is a term that Harris favors over the term postindustrial society. As do I.

5. The debate over "infrastructural determinism" was a running battle between Harris and his critics. In a personal communication to me (November 15, 1998) he had this to say: "Like many of my critics, you have been bothered by the possibility (if not certainty) that I have slighted the influence of structural and superstructural features. Perhaps the enclosed new book of mine [*Theories of Culture in Postmodern Times*] will help you see that when a distinction between long- and short-term causality is introduced, seemingly independent and idealist relationships fall under the control of the infrastructure" (para . 4).

6. Like the majority of anthropologists, most of Harris's writings concern more traditional societies such as hunting and gathering or horticultural.

7. Harris points out that hunting and gathering people had several techniques to control their population. One of the milder methods is "prolonged lactation" which consists of prolonging the nursing of infants. It seems that, among women whose diets are high in protein and low in carbohydrates, a diet typical of hunters and gatherers, lactation leads to lower fertility. Prolonging the nursing process for three or four years will thus allow the woman to have some control over the spacing of her children (Harris, 1971, pp. 24–25). As uncontrolled human fertility has the potential to double population size every twenty-five years, prolonged lactation and other more active and harsher methods must have been used to keep population levels in line with what the environment could provide. Harris points out that even a .5 percent growth rate (doubling every 139 years) sustained for just the last 10,000 years of the hunting and gathering era would be devastating. Even with such low growth rate, "by 10,000 B.C. the population of the earth would have reached 604,463,000,000,000,000,000,000" (Harris, 1971, p. 25). Shades of Malthus, indeed.

8. Jared Diamond, in *Guns, Germs, and Steel* (1997) later elaborates on these differences and their subsequent historical impact.

9. In fact, so rich are the wild grains of the Middle East that permanent settlements probably precede the domestication of plants and animals (1971, p. 178). Harris asserts that as the result of the domestication of plants and animals,

human population in the Near East explodes. "Beginning with 100,000 people in 8000 B.C., the population of the Middle East probably reached 3.2 million shortly before 4000 B.C.—a fortyfold increase in 4,000 years" (1977, p. 43). This population increase, of course, puts pressure on the society to further intensify production with all its consequent impacts on the environment.

10. Harris points out that it took approximately 2,000 years to turn teosinte, a wild grain that grows in the highlands of Mexico, into domesticated varieties of maize. At first the cobs were "less than an inch long and had just a few rows of tiny kernels, which were easily dislodged at harvest time" (1989, pp. 475–476). It was only by about 1000 B.C. when selective breeding allowed corn to reach its modern dimensions with the kernels firmly on the cob for human harvest (and completely reliant on human planting). The wild wheat of the Middle East, by contrast, is far closer to domesticated varieties. In terms of animal domesticates, Harris points out that the Americas did eventually domesticate turkeys, and dogs in the Mexican highlands, but these cannot compare to the Old World cattle. South America did, of course, have the llamas and the guinea pig—but again these are not important sources of meat or traction.

11. Harris (1977, pp. 31–34) briefly considers Paul C. Martin's hypothesis that the big game animals (including horses) were all killed by American Indians shortly after arriving on the continent from Siberia. Martin (and others since) attributed this to the fact that these large animals had never before encountered humans and consequently were relatively easy prey when the first Americans crossed the Bering land bridge 11,000 years ago. While such a scenario fits in well with his overall theory, Harris doubts this because of some evidence that humans made the crossing well before that date. Today, however, the evidence of an earlier date for the settlement of the Americas is very much in doubt.

12. Harris, like Malthus, is not an advocate of doom predicting the ultimate depletion of all natural resources. For Harris (like Malthus), depletion is ongoing, usually offset by intensifying technology or changing the resources upon which a society is based. In *America Now* he criticizes environmentalists who spread such gloom and doom: "The central fallacy of the new dismal science is that it interprets the present crisis in the light of a future crisis. Perhaps depletion of natural resources will indeed drag us down into an entropic death. But why impose a distant morbid possibility on a present that is still pregnant with life and hope?" (1981, p. 176).

13. It was *America Now*, at least in 1981 the year it was published. Since that time globalization has thrust American industry back into a competitive environment which changes a few details of Harris's analysis. However, the bulk of the analysis holds up rather well. It was also *America Now* when it was originally published. The book was later republished under the title *Why Nothing Works*, "Harris's original choice for the title" (Margolis and Kottak, 2003, p. 688).

14. Harris's analysis of the growth and centralization of corporations and governments is fine as far as it goes. However, it fails to identify any infrastruc-

tural reasons for this centralization! Capitalism is a structural factor. Keynesian theory is part of the superstructure. Governments and corporations have grown around the world in the twentieth century, not just in the United States. Harris fails to cite ongoing environmental depletion, pollution, more complicated production and distribution processes to offset these environmental effects, or changes in population size and composition as factors in the growth of corporate and government structures. There are structural causes of government growth that Harris fails to mention as well, including the needs of the military (which dominates U.S. Government growth in terms of personnel and is significant in terms of spending), the rise of interest group politics, and the role of elites.

15. Consider the lily. A lily seed from space lands in a farmer's pond. It sprouts a flower that doubles in size every day. It takes nineteen days for the lily to cover half the pond. How many days till it covers the whole pond? This, of course, is a riddle of exponential growth. When something grows exponentially, actual physical growth depends not only on the rate of change but also the level or size it has already attained. In the case of the lily, the rate of change is 100 percent per day. If it takes nineteen days to cover half the pond, it will only take an additional day to cover the other half.

16. The growth of GDP since World War II has simply been phenomenal. In 1946 the Gross Domestic Product of the United States totaled 222.3 billion dollars, or 1.6 triilion in constant 2000 dollars. By 2000 U.S. GDP stood at $9.8 trillion, an economy producing six times the value of goods and services.

17. The number of workers in manufacturing occupations has only increased slightly during this time, so the rise in product must in large part be a result of increasing productivity by the American worker. This is achieved through the application of technology, squeezing wages, tighter organization and monitoring of the workforce, and increasing the detailed division of labor.

18. Why hasn't American manufacturing growth kept pace with the other sectors of the economy? Perhaps the major reason is increasing imports of manufactured goods from abroad, and increasing competition from other nations in export markets as well, or globalization. Of the major sectors of the economy, manufacturing and agriculture are perhaps the most susceptible to competition from other nations. Also, American manufacturing corporations—in search of lower labor costs and more "favorable" environmental, tax, and worker safety laws—are locating more of their operations overseas. While some services can be "out-sourced" or be provided from anywhere through fiber optic lines or satellite, many services rely heavily on language, culture, and/or geographic location. Again, manufacturing is not so restricted.

19. According to Miller there are two other factors responsible for economic growth. The first is "total capital" (physical capital such as tools and machines and human capital or the amount of knowledge gained from research and education) which he estimates accounts for one third of the growth rate in per capita income. The other factor is an increase in productivity that Miller believes is responsible for the remaining portion of economic growth.

20. You should note that this theory is straight out of Malthus, with its cost/benefit analysis based on the competition for resources affecting birth rates. It is therefore highly compatible with Harris's cultural materialism.

21. An investment tip for the coming decade: hospitals, nursing homes, mortuaries, and cemeteries.

22. The growing dependence of the middle class on bureaucracies, of course, was also a theme of C. Wright Mills.

3

Wallerstein's World-Systems Analysis

Wallerstein is not advocating a new theory in sociology; rather he is advocating a whole new way of doing social science. The focus of social science, Wallerstein believes, is tied much too closely to the nation-state or, more vaguely, to "society." He asserts that states as well as the organizations and groups that make up such structures exist within a much broader economic, political, and legal framework he calls "world-systems" (Wallerstein, 1974, p. 5). World-systems, according to Wallerstein, are the only true social system—they alone contain all social relations that are necessary for survival, they alone comprise the complete division of labor necessary for sustenance and growth. Nation-states must be understood in terms of the world context of their era, and modern nation-states can only be fully understood in terms of the modern world-system of capitalism. It is thus world-systems that are the proper subject of the social sciences (Wallerstein, 2000, p. 125).

It is the complete division of labor that is regularly reproduced that Wallerstein takes as the defining boundary of a historical social system (Wallerstein, 2000, p. 139). A total social system must be able to meet all of the essential needs of the substantial majority of people through production and economic exchange within the system itself (Wallerstein, 2000, pp. 74–75). It is not necessary to share the same political structure or culture to accomplish this economic exchange, only that the essential needs of "sustenance, protection and pleasure" be met by a single, interdependent division of labor (Wallerstein, 2000, p. 82).

By this definition, there have only been three basic types of social systems throughout history. The first are well studied by anthropologists, what Wallerstein terms as "mini-systems." These are small in size, homogenous, relatively simple in structure (Wallerstein, 2000, p. 139). When Wallerstein also states that such societies are characterized by "reciprocity in exchanges," he is obviously referring to such self-contained sociocultural systems as hunting and gathering societies and perhaps simple horticultural, herding, and fishing societies. Such systems are no more.

The other two types of systems are "world-systems," which Wallerstein defines as a single division of labor but spanning multiple cultures (Wallerstein, 2000, p. 75). There are two types of these, one with a unified political system, which Wallerstein terms a "world- empire," and one without, or a "world-economy" (Wallerstein, 2000, p. 75). The key characteristic of the economy of a world-empire is that it is based on extracting the surplus from outlying districts (rural producers) through a small number of government and religious officials. Part of this tribute goes to maintain the small number of functionaries who extract the tribute, part must go to maintain the military to ensure continued domination, and the rest goes to the rulers at the center (Wallerstein, 1974, p. 16; 2000, p. 139). While reliable, such political tribute comes at the high cost of political administration and military force to both extract the tribute and provide protection to these outlying areas. Wallerstein adds that such empires undergo constant expansion and contraction over their lifespan (and can be quite vast at the height of their expansion). Such world-empires have existed since ancient times and have continued (in somewhat modified form) right up to the present.

Wallerstein calls the third type of historical system "world-economies" and characterizes this type by the systemic and complete division of labor, containing all of the necessary units to reproduce the necessities of life ("vast uneven chains of integrated production structures") as well as a lack of a centralized political unit ("dissected by multiple political structures") (Wallerstein, 2000, p. 139). World economies, Wallerstein adds, are usually short lived and weak— quickly disintegrating, becoming conquered by world-empires, or transformed into a world-empire by the political expansion of one of its constituent states after only a brief life span (Wallerstein, 2000, p. 140).

In about 1500, for unique historical reasons, one world-economy managed to survive and develop. The capitalist world-system began in Europe and, pushed by an imperative to accumulate capital, by the late nineteenth century covered the globe. In the process the expanding capitalist world-system absorbed mini-systems, world-empires, and competing world-economies (Wallerstein, 2000, p. 140). Modernity itself is defined by the increasing dominance of this world-system; it is one of the two major watersheds of human history, a fundamental change that has transformed the world (Wallerstein, 1974, p. 3).[1] Our times are defined by a single capitalist world-economy which forms the context in which the struggles between nations, classes, races, ethnic groups, and political movements are decided.

Wallerstein insists that the great theoretical and methodological debates within the social sciences revolve around the question of how best to understand and account for the qualitative differences between the premodern and the modern worlds (Wallerstein, 1974, p. 3–4). He advocates world-systems as the proper unit of analysis for building and testing theories of social stability and change. But he does not stop there; he urges other changes in the practice of social science to better explain the stability and evolution of human social systems.

For example, Wallerstein urges social scientists to drop the distinction between history and social science or more specifically, to stop the specialization within either idiographic or nomothetic methodologies. Nomothetic scholarship is patterned after the natural sciences and is based on the search for the general laws of human behavior and society.[2] Such laws, it was envisaged, would be timeless and would cut across all types of societies. This rapidly became the method of choice among the disciplines of economics, sociology, and political science (Wallerstein, 2000, p. 150). Idiographic scholarship, on the other hand, insists that there were no natural laws in society, that social reality was always tied to a specific time and place. This rapidly became the dominant methodology of history and anthropology as both disciplines endeavored to reconstruct empirical reality.[3] Wallerstein advocates both methods as valid and necessary in studying historical social systems (Wallerstein, 2000, p. 151). All social analysis worthy of the name must be rooted in history and informed by theory, has to be nomothetic and idiographic, "historic and systemic" (Wallerstein, 2000, p. xvii).

In his writings he practices both methods simultaneously as well. Thus a sociologist will find much of his scholarship strongly idiographic, meticulously detailing the rise and operation of the capitalist world-system through specific events, times, and places. An historian would no doubt find his work extremely nomothetic, writing of a stable, yet evolving, core and periphery areas; the rise and fall of hegemonic states; economic cycles, as well as the predicted decline of the capitalist world-system, all processes that span centuries if not millennia.

Wallerstein seeks to further change the way we practice social science by calling on the adoption of a "unidisciplinary approach" (Wallerstein, 1974, p. 11). He advocates abandoning the traditional specializations of economics, political science, sociology, anthropology, and history. In the case of political science, economics, and sociology, each discipline has taken a part of "society" as its own special province. History and the other social sciences, of course, have divided the subject matter between past and present. Anthropology has divided the subject matter by place (Western vs. non-Western). These divisions, Wallerstein argues, are consistent with a vision of the social system as a single nation state or society. They are consistent with a nineteenth century ideology that sees each area—state, market, society, and culture—as analytically separate and distinct (Wallerstein, 2000, p. 133). They are nearly useless if we take as our unit of analysis the study of world-systems that span the globe and historical time. Wallerstein asserts that there are far more differences in terms of subject matter, method, and theories within these "disciplines" than between them (Wallerstein, 2000, p. 133). Far from serving to further our understanding of the world these specializations stand in the way of our analysis. Political, economic, social, and cultural variables are interrelated in many complex ways; no very useful model[4] can exclusively focus upon factors within a single discipline (Wallerstein, 2000, p. 134). Wallerstein views social science as "a single discipline" and therefore calls upon us to "restructure the social sciences as a whole" (Wallerstein, 2000, p. 170). "In my view, what is necessary is a complete overhaul of the boundaries. None of the three present cleavages is plausible or desirable. The distinction past/present is totally without merit. The distinction West/non-West must be fundamentally rethought. The distinction state/market/civil society must be abolished" (Wallerstein, 2000, p. 182).

One distinction within the social sciences which may have some relevance, Wallerstein allows, is the distinction between micro and macro levels of analysis (Wallerstein, 2000, p. 182). He goes on to report a very curious fact. A look at the work of the classical writers in each of the disciplines reveals that they tended to be very macro in scope, taking on very large themes such as evolution, social transformation, and stages of civilization (Wallerstein, 2000, p. 192). However, this macro focus did not last too long. In the interests of establishing themselves as disciplines,[5] they turned to specialization and away from macro scholarship. "As originality required that each successive scholar say something new, and the easiest way to do that was to divide up the subject matter into subjects of ever smaller scope" (Wallerstein, 2000, pp. 192–193). This, as well as the demands of the state and economy to use social science as a tool of rational reform, led scholars to a level of hyperspecialization at the microscopic level and away from macro social theory (Wallerstein, 2000, p. 170; pp. 193–195).[6] Wallerstein, of course, is a strong advocate of macro analysis, an advocacy that again sets him apart from mainstream social science (Wallerstein, 2000, p. 109).

Wallerstein also challenges mainstream social scientists to become committed to social justice. Such commitment need not jeopardize our obligation to objectivity. Like others, social scientists belong to a wide range of groups that demand allegiance and socialize their members into values, beliefs, and attitudes toward the social world. These groups are all inter-related to one another, often in competition. "Since we all belong to multiple groups, we often have to make decisions as to the priorities demanded by our loyalties. Scholars and scientists are not somehow exempt from this requirement" (Wallerstein, 1974, p. 9). Wallerstein argues that we need to explicitly recognize that we are a part of the social world and that our memberships in groups as well as placement within social structures—and thus our subsequent values, standards, and beliefs—may well tax our objectivity as social scientists. By pretending that we are not so affected, Wallerstein maintains, we are setting ourselves up for becoming irrelevant, mere social technicians, or apologists for the status quo (Wallerstein, 2000, p. 195).

But we also must recognize that the subject matter of all of the social sciences is of critical importance to the groups, institutions, and states of the modern world-system. Recounting the subject matter of the social sciences is itself a social act—even the recounting of the past affects the present, its constituent institutions, groups, nation states and system as a whole (Wallerstein, 1974, p. 9). "Social reality is ephemeral. It exists in the present and disappears as it moves into the past. The past can only be told as it truly is, not was. For recounting the past is a social act of the present done by men of the present and affecting the social system of the present. 'Truth' changes because society changes" (Wallerstein, 1974, p. 9). The subject matter of the social sciences is notoriously open to interpretation, and again, interpretation is subject to the social scientist's memberships and placement in various structures.

The role of the social scientist is to discern social reality within the framework of these commitments and to recount them as best we can. This should be done with a recognition that certain groups are not well represented among the ranks of social scientists, and thus the field cannot be truly objective, results must therefore be "biased" toward groups that are well represented and against those that are not. The task must also be performed in the recognition that there are elite groups that will find the elaboration of social reality threatening to their positions of dominance, and that, because of their political, social, and economic power, will exert pressure on social scientists to avert their gaze. It is because of these inherent limitations of social science that we must commit ourselves to a more egalitarian, libertarian, and socially just world. To attain that, we must be clear on the present structure and evolution of the capitalist world-system, and of "the range of possible developments in the present and the future. That kind of knowledge would be power. And within the framework of my commitments, it would be a power that would be most useful to those groups which represent the interests of the larger and more oppressed parts of the world's population" (Wallerstein, 1974, p. 10).

THE CAPITALIST WORLD-SYSTEM

Within the overall structure of the capitalist world-system, Wallerstein examines the impact of conflict and cooperation among class, ethnic, racial, gender, and national groups.[7] It is within the world-system context that he examines social, economic, and political institutions, international organizations, capitalist enterprises, and nation states that make up the system. It is within the world-system context that he looks at the differing impact of long-running economic cycles that affect the economic and political fortunes of nation states around the world, as well as the rise and fall of great powers. Because of the arrow of time, the social world is extremely complex. In fact, Wallerstein claims, human social systems are the most complex structures in the universe (Wallerstein, 2000, p. 197). As with any system, everything affects everything else, and through time, everything expands, divides, and multiplies—nothing is eliminated, all is cumulative. But, Wallerstein hastens to add, this is not to say that the social world is unpredictable. "It is a child of its own past, which has created the parameters within which these new paths are chosen" (Wallerstein, 2000, p. 197).[8] For very short and very long time spans, Wallerstein maintains, the social world appears to be determined; free will seems to reign in the "vast intermediate zone" of social life (Wallerstein, 2000, p. 201).

Like all systems, he maintains, human social systems are composed of parts that fit together in "provisional orderly patterns, self-established, holding things together, creating seeming coherence" (Wallerstein, 2000, p. 197). But these patterns never long endure; there are "internal contradictions" within and among the constituent parts of any system that through the passage of time move the various parts further and further away from this temporary order. "These evolving structures repeatedly reach points at which their equilibria can no longer be restored, at points of bifurcation, and then new paths are found, new orders established, but we can never know in advance what these new orders will be" (Wallerstein, 2000, p. 197). Wallerstein believes that the internal contradictions of the capitalist world-system have reached a crisis stage—we are at a point of bifurcation. We must rapidly develop a social science capable of comprehending and guiding us through these developments, a social science that will enable us to achieve a more just and egalitarian world. Such a world will only come about, Wallerstein argues, through human agency acting on the development of such knowledge. To promote this he advocates a whole new field of social science that he calls "utopistics." By *utopistics* Wallerstein means the serious study of possible futures, the positing of alternative future social organization and assessing the attainability, sustainability, advantages, and limitations of these alternatives. It is the explicit application of social science theory and method to exploring substantively rational[9] and attainable futures.

It is important to grasp that Wallerstein does not view the modern world-system as being due to the slow development of local European economies to first national status and then, gradually, to encompass the world. Rather, the world-economy was created first by establishing long-distance trade in bulk goods and linking production processes worldwide—raw materials, food, fuel, and later manufactured goods all became a part of these "commodity chains" allowing the accumulation of significant profit to European capitalists (Wallerstein, 2000, p. 121). With the establishment of capitalism, the modern nation state was created to foster and protect capitalist development, first in Europe and then throughout the world. It was the expansion of capitalism that fostered the growth of the interstate system, the sovereignty of nations, and the rise of nationalism. "Hence, slowly, and more or less coordinate with the evolving boundaries of each state, a corresponding nationalist sentiment took root. The modern world-system has developed from one in which these 'nationalisms' were weak or nonexistent to one in which they were salient, well-ensconced, and pervasive" (Wallerstein, 2000, p. 122). Other social groups were also fostered by the growth of the capitalist world-system, including social classes and household structures. "In all of this description, the imagery I am employing is not of a small core adding on outer layers but a thin outer framework gradually filling in a dense inner network" (Wallerstein, 2000, p. 122).

As conceived by Wallerstein, the capitalist world-economy that results from the crisis of European feudalism is something truly revolutionary. It is a mechanism of surplus appropriation that is both subtle and highly efficient. It is a method which rejects the extraction of tribute by force (as in empires), or of the collection of rents (as in feudalism) but instead relies on the creation of surplus through constantly expanding productivity, and through surplus extraction through the creation of profit (Wallerstein, 1974, pp. 37–38). The goal of capitalism is to produce goods and services for sale in a market and to maximize profit. It is structured to reward those who innovate and develop new products or more profitable ways of producing old products (Wallerstein, 2000, p. 83).[10] Finally, it is a system that establishes itself worldwide. This is accomplished first through the creation of a worldwide division of labor in which different classes and status groups are given differential access to resources within nations; and second, through the creation of a world-market in which goods and services are sold, a market very much distorted by the power (and lack of power) of individual nation states that make up the political units of this world-economy (Wallerstein, 1974, pp. 37–38).

Wallerstein's view of capitalism is not the standard fare of social science textbooks. For Wallerstein, capitalism was truly a "world-system" phenomenon from the beginning (Wallerstein, 2000, p. 87). By definition, a world-economy is far larger than any one political entity. Held together by network of economic trade a world economy contains a variety of political units (nation-states, colonies, empires) within its scope (Wallerstein, 1974, p. 15). Wallerstein's posited relationships between the capitalist world-system and these political units are fascinating. To begin with, the modern nation states, as well as the interstate system itself, evolved within the context of a pre-existing capitalist economy; that is, the capitalist world-system first established trade and integrated production processes across vast regions, and state and local political units then developed within this context (Wallerstein, 1974, p. 67; 2000, p. 222). Wallerstein also posits that these cross-cutting political units have become essential for significant capital accumulation.

For Wallerstein, the division of labor isn't just internal to a nation-state or other political unit that is based on occupation, race, sex, class, or ethnicity. It is also geographical between political units (Wallerstein, 1974, p. 349; 2000, p. 86). Wallerstein divides the capitalist world-economy into core states, semi-peripheral, and peripheral areas. The peripheral areas are least developed; they are exploited by the core for their cheap labor, raw materials, and agricultural production. The semi-periphery is an intermediate zone, containing some manufacturing, particularly in those industries that are no longer very profitable. Outside of the capitalist world-economy are "external areas" that consist of areas that have limited trade relations with the world-system or those areas that are completely isolated. External areas have been shrinking over the last 500 years as world capitalism has expanded around the globe.

The core states are in geographically advantaged areas of the world. For historical and geographical reasons, these states have strong state machinery and the political power to enforce unequal rates of exchange upon peripheral areas; such unequal exchanges are a significant source of capital accumulation in private hands. The state also promotes capital accumulation through trade barriers and quotas, government purchasing, tax policy, legal constraints on trade, and establishing and regulating patents—again these near monopoly rights granted by the state are a significant source of capital accumulation (Wallerstein, 1999, p. 64). The state also plays a role in capital accumulation through maintaining social order through minimizing class struggle through force, manipulation, and the creation of the welfare state (Wallerstein, 1999, p. 66).[11] Finally, the state assists the maximization of private capital by absorbing many of the environmental, research and development, and infrastructural costs (such as roads, sewers, airports) of production (Wallerstein, 1999, pp. 80–85).

Wallerstein considers it axiomatic that within the capitalist world-system core areas will have relatively strong political structures—that is, they will be militarily and economically strong with a population that is very nationalistic and culturally integrated (Wallerstein, 1974, p. 349). Such strength serves the interests of key elites in the protection and justification of economic and political inequalities caused by the world-system (Wallerstein, 1974, p. 349). If all governments were equally strong, Wallerstein argues, they would then effectively block significant capital accumulation of groups located in other states. "It would then follow that the world division of labor would be impeded, the world-economy would decline, and eventually the world-system would fall apart (Wallerstein, 1974, pp. 354–355). If no state were strong, on the other hand, capitalist elites would have no political mechanism to assist in the accumulation of capital—having to depend on a free market would truly be disastrous for significant capital accumulation (Wallerstein, 1974, p. 355). What evolves, therefore, are core areas in which the states are far more powerful than others in periphery and semiperiphery areas. These core states can then enforce the unequal division of labor and exploitative exchange rates throughout the world-system (Wallerstein, 1974, p. 355).

The core states are those with the most vibrant, complex, and profitable economic institutions. It is only when such industries lose their monopoly status and become far less profitable that they are allowed to develop in peripheral or semiperipheral areas. This was true of the steel and textile industries of an earlier industrial era. It is equally true of the industries of this era as well (Wallerstein, 1999, pp. 43–44). The division of labor is worldwide, core states having a far higher proportion of skilled and semiskilled workers to go along with their industries (Wallerstein, 1974, p. 350). To some extent this division of labor between core and periphery is based on history and location. But to a much larger extent, Wallerstein claims, it is based on "the social organization of work, one which magnifies and legitimizes the ability of some groups within the system to exploit the labor of others, that is, to receive a larger share of the surplus" (Wallerstein, 1974, p. 349). The main way this is done is through the development of strong states in the core areas which enforce unequal exchange on periphery areas (Wallerstein, 2000, p. 86). "The functioning then of a capitalist world-economy requires that groups pursue their economic interests within a single world market while seeking to distort this market for their benefit by organizing to exert influence on states, some of which are far more powerful than others but none of which controls the world-market in its entirety" (Wallerstein, 2000, p. 92). Market forces, of course, which tend to reward both capital and skilled/educated labor, serve to perpetuate the disparities. The economic, political, and social polarization caused by the world-wide division of labor is increasing (Wallerstein, 1999, p. 44).

Wallerstein claims that the advantages of the core states in the capitalist world-system are enormous and that their power and wealth have expanded significantly throughout the evolution of the system. However, the system is dynamic: Core states can lose their status over time (Wallerstein, 1974, p. 350). States have what Wallerstein terms a "tipping mechanism" in which initial strength can suddenly become magnified or a small weakness can suddenly bring a system crashing down. For example, "The tax revenue enables the state to have a larger and more efficient bureaucracy and army, which in turn leads to greater tax revenue—a process that continues in spiral form" (Wallerstein, 1974, p. 356). It is through this mechanism that small changes within systems can sometimes produce large results. We will revisit this "tipping theory" when dealing with Wallerstein's analysis of "hegemonic" powers, nation states that Wallerstein defines as truly dominant in particular eras.

Unlike traditional Marxists, Wallerstein does not consider the state to be a mere front for capitalist interests. Once established, government officials have their own interests and agendas. Such officials want to continue in power as well as increase their personal wealth and prestige (Wallerstein, 1999, p. 67). In addition, Wallerstein adds, creating a strong state involves making "constitutional compromises" with other interests, and these may very well conflict with the interests of capital (Wallerstein, 2000, p. 88). While they certainly have to satisfy the capitalist class, they must also garner support among workers, retirees, evangelicals, and other voters. Such appeals are necessary to give the state legitimacy, a necessary stabilizer of modern government (Wallerstein, 1999, p. 67). However, promises and policies to attract some voters may sometimes come into conflict with the interests of economic elites (Wallerstein, 2000, p. 88). Wallerstein believes that capitalists are very powerful in the present world-system, but they are not all-powerful nor do they always get their way (Wallerstein, 1999, p. 67).

Wallerstein views the modern nation-state as a recent phenomenon, quite different from the state structures that existed in non-capitalist systems (Wallerstein, 1999, pp. 59–60). Foremost among the differences is the claim of sovereignty. This is a claim that all matters within the boundaries of the state are the province of that state. A sovereign state may pursue whatever policies it chooses, and no one inside the state has the right to refuse to obey these laws. A claim of sovereignty within an interstate system means that nation-states also give up the right to interfere with the internal policies of other states as well (Wallerstein, 1999, p. 60). Sovereignty within the interstate system involves reciprocal recognition of this right by other sovereign states. Wallerstein adds, of course, that some states are more powerful than others, both internally and within the interstate system (Wallerstein, 1999, p. 61).

CAPITALIST WORLD-SYSTEM STABILITY AND CHANGE

Like any historical system, Wallerstein states, the capitalist world-system had a beginning—a formative period in which it expanded and incorporated more and more areas of the world—and one day it will disintegrate and cease to be (Wallerstein, 2000, p. 271). As stated previously, the origin of capitalism occurs in the long sixteenth century (i.e., 1450 to 1650); while capitalism begins in Western Europe, it quickly expands to the Spanish and Portuguese colonies of the Americas in the opening centuries. The second stage goes from about 1750 to 1850, in which the Russian and Ottoman Empires were brought into the system, as well as southern Asia, west Africa, and the rest of the Americas. In the third great expansion (1850–1900) the rest of the world was incorporated—Oceania, East Asia, and the rest of Africa. At this point, and to the present day, world capitalism was truly global, bringing the entire world within a single division of labor (Wallerstein, 1999, p. 58). Industrial production becomes an ever larger proportion of total world production (Wallerstein, 2000, p. 94). Access to raw materials to support this production becomes more essential; transportation of goods and raw materials becomes more efficient and economically viable; improved military capabilities of the core states in relation to the periphery make the necessary exploitation more effective (Wallerstein, 2000, p. 94).

How can such an unequal system maintain itself? Why don't the exploited, who constitute the vast majority of humankind, simply revolt against the small minority of capitalists? (Wallerstein, 2000, p. 89–90). One reason revolution is difficult is that there is no central institution or government responsible for the disparities. Such an institution would serve to focus discontent. Nor is there a single institution to which one could appeal that could serve to counteract the inequalities (Wallerstein, 1974, p. 350). The extreme economic disparities between core and periphery[12] are due to a capitalist world-economy, an entity that is extremely difficult to identify, blame, communicate with, or to march against.

There are also three mechanisms identified by Wallerstein by which the capitalist world-system maintains political stability. The first is the existence of a semiperiphery. The "semiperiphery" areas are states that are intermediate between periphery and core in terms of the complexity of their economy and in the strength of their governments and military (Wallerstein, 1974, p. 349). Some of these are former core states in decline, others former peripheral areas that are on the rise—the capitalist world-system is dynamic and ever changing. The middle areas serve to absorb or deflect much of the political pressure coming from the peripheral areas for fundamental change of the system (Wallerstein, 1974, p. 350). It is a way of dividing potential opposition into a large lower strata which is completely exploited, and a smaller middle strata that receives limited economic benefits and concessions (Wallerstein, 2000, p. 90). It provides political stability by preventing a complete polarization between the elites and everybody else. "The existence of the third category means precisely that the upper stratum is not faced with the unified opposition of all the others, because the middle stratum is both exploited and exploiter" (Wallerstein, 2000, p. 91).

The second is the overwhelming military force of the core states. Military force, or the threat of it, is a great stabilizer both internally and internationally (Wallerstein, 2000, p. 90). However, force is expensive to maintain, and it can serve to coalesce opposition. There are more efficient ways to keep a population loyal to the state (Wallerstein, 1999, p. 66).

The third, and perhaps most important basis of political stability, is an ideology that commits the population of the world-system to the system itself (Wallerstein, 2000, p. 90). Wallerstein asserts that this ideology is one of economic progress and development based on liberal reform of state structures. Between 1848 (when Europe was wracked by leftist revolutions) and 1917 (the Russian Revolution) Western political leaders began a series of reforms designed to curb some of the worst abuses of capitalism and more fully integrate their populations into the nation state (Wallerstein, 1999, p. 9). Three main strategies were developed. First, suffrage was extended from a small propertied class to all adult males and eventually females living within the state. The second strategy was the establishment of the welfare state: workplace legislation to curb some of the worst labor abuses as well as the creation of an income safety net, social security, and other redistributive programs. The third method of integrating populations into the nation-state was the strengthening of nationalism and national loyalty through compulsory education and universal military service. These three reforms become standard practice of the liberal state, which by the early twentieth century become the norm for the core states of the capitalist world-system (Wallerstein, 1999, p. 9).

From 1848 to 1968 liberal ideology—the reform of state apparatus to soften some of the worst abuses of capitalism—was the dominant ideology of the West (Wallerstein, 1999, pp. 38–39). The ideologies of conservatism and radicalism were merely variants on this theme, advocating essentially a different pace of reform (Wallerstein, 1999, p. 39). During this period liberalism and its variants created an enormous amount of optimism about the future. Faith in progress, both technological and political, meant that people could tolerate inequality, poverty, and political powerlessness because it was widely believed that tomorrow would be a better day, that our children would live richer and freer (Wallerstein, 1999, pp. 17–18). This faith was widely questioned in the world-wide political turmoil of 1968 and has been weakening ever since. This loss of faith in liberal reform is being encouraged by a "resurgent" conservative movement, which sees opportunity for dismantling redistributive programs, lowering taxes, and re-creating an earlier (and more profitable) version of capitalism. But Wallerstein does not see these conservative movements as the cause of the loss of faith, only as exploiting it. Rather, the loss of faith was due to the failure of liberalism to seriously address fundamental inequalities caused by the capitalist world-system. Even when in control of state structures, neither reformers nor self-styled radicals could operate outside the structures of the capitalist world-system.

One consequence of this weakening of faith in progress is the withdrawal of popular support for the state, a loss of faith in government as a solution for social problems (Wallerstein, 1999, p. 45). This sets the stage for both further social, political, and economic polarization within nation-states as well as an overall weakening of the power of nation states. People begin to question, not only the state's role in the economy, but the efficiency and use of its military and security forces, the effectiveness and desirability of virtually all government programs (Wallerstein, 1999, p. 45). The strong state, you will recall, is a key component in maintaining the profitability and viability of economic enterprises headquartered in core countries. Strong core states, within a well-defined interstate system, are absolutely essential for the long-term maintenance of the capitalist world-system. Their weakening, Wallerstein believes, will have devastating consequences for the world-system as a whole.

For Wallerstein, the twentieth century was a period of consolidation of the capitalist world-system. This fourth stage also saw the establishment of multiple regimes around the world calling themselves socialist, with an ideology that directly challenged capitalism (Wallerstein, 2000, p. 97). For Wallerstein, however, socialism has never truly existed; all states are part of the capitalist world-system. True socialism cannot exist without encompassing a single division of labor, a single world-economy and perhaps a single world-government (Wallerstein, 2000, p. 102).[13] The establishment of nation-states calling themselves socialist served to depolarize the world through creating a semi-periphery (the "communist bloc") of state-directed industrialization. This semi-periphery not only rapidly expanded industrial production in former peripheral areas, it also served to redistribute a larger share of the newly created surplus to their populations (Wallerstein, 2000, pp. 100–101). This is a period of consolidation for the capitalist world-system because this "triad of strata" (core, semiperiphery, and periphery) is a mainstay in the survival of the world-system. The existence of a communist bloc has also been a useful foil for U.S. hegemony in the latter half of the twentieth century.

According to Wallerstein, the whole capitalist economic world-system is based on core state exploitation of the periphery. But the states within the core are not a single unit. Rather, the nation states of the core are in rivalry with each other for political, economic, and military dominance. One can think of the state of this rivalry as existing on a continuum, with one end being roughly equal powers with no clear, long-lasting groupings or alliances between them. The other end of the continuum is one in which one nation becomes so powerful in economic, military, and political matters that it achieves almost total dominance in world affairs (Wallerstein, 2000, p. 255).[14] Wallerstein posits that a nation-state achieves hegemony when its economic and military power becomes enormous in comparison to the other core states. Once achieved, the hegemonic power largely dominates international relations. It achieves this status through the efficiency and productivity of its agricultural and industrial production, commerce and finance (Wallerstein, 2000, p. 255).

There have been only three hegemonic powers in the history of the capitalist world-system. The first was the United Provinces (the present day Netherlands) in the middle of the seventeenth century, the second was the United Kingdom in the middle of the nineteenth, and the third is the U.S. after World War II (Wallerstein, 2000, p. 256). Wallerstein posits that hegemonic powers achieve dominance in each of these areas in order (agricultural, manufacturing, commerce, and finance), and that as they lose their hegemonic status, they lose dominance in these areas in this order as well (Wallerstein, 2000, p. 257). In addition to the sequencing of acquiring and losing dominance, he posits other parallels between the three hegemonic powers. Each attains hegemonic status after a long struggle (a "thirty years war") with a rival power (Wallerstein, 2000, p. 437).[15] At its height, each hegemonic power becomes a strong advocate of free trade and liberalism. Each were sea powers (or in America's case, sea and air) and were somewhat hesitant to develop and then to deploy large armies during their rise to hegemonic status (Wallerstein, 2000, pp. 256–258). Hegemonic states function to keep order among the nation states, as well as to interfere in the "market" to benefit producers within its borders (Wallerstein, 2000, p. 435). This interference tends to be cumulative, building up huge surpluses for its enterprises, thus providing the state with resources to further extend its power (Wallerstein, 2000, p. 260–261).

Wallerstein posits that the United States is, of course, in the process of losing its hegemonic status.[16] Like all institutions and systems, hegemony contains contradictions that eventually work themselves out to qualitatively change the system. What are the internal contradictions that are causing America's decline? Global liberalism, championed by the United States after World War II to promote the free flow of raw materials, goods, and peoples makes it impossible to contain the spread of technological expertise. "Hence over time it is virtually inevitable that entrepreneurs coming along later will be able to enter the most profitable markets with the most advanced technologies and younger 'plant,' thus eating into the material base of the productivity edge of the hegemonic power" (Wallerstein, 2000, p. 261). A second contradiction is the rise of income of the workers and managers of the enterprises within the hegemonic power. Over time the hegemonic nation loses its competitive edge (Wallerstein, 2000, pp. 261–262). Finally, hegemonic powers bear an enormous military burden; this cost in money and manpower must eventually undermine its economy (Wallerstein, 2000, p. 437).

The rise and decline of a hegemonic power is merely one of several cyclical processes of capitalism. Another cyclical feature of the capitalist world-system is "Kondratieff waves," economic cycles of expansion and contraction that are some 50 to 60 years in length. These cyclical processes have been a part of the world-system from the beginning and are part of the normal functioning of the world-system. However, Wallerstein asserts, there are other changes that threaten the continuance of the system itself, and it is to these changes that we now turn.

THE DECLINE AND FALL OF THE
CAPITALIST WORLD-SYSTEM

The decline and fall of capitalism, Wallerstein suggests, lies in three elemental features of the system that are essential in sustaining and expanding the accumulation of capital. The first is that the capitalist system must constantly expand production and markets. This expansion is both geographical and in terms of production; the system must constantly bring in new markets and new workers into its orbit. The second feature of the system is that the most successful capitalists are those who externalize many of their production costs. Wallerstein calls this capitalism's "dirty little secret"—they don't pay all their bills (Wallerstein, 1999, pp. 77–78). The third and final feature of the system, strongly related to the second feature, is that the nation-state and the interstate system is an integral part of the process of capital accumulation (Wallerstein, 1999, p. 74). Despite the official antistate rhetoric, Wallerstein asserts, state power used on behalf of capital is absolutely essential for the functioning of the world-system (Wallerstein, 1999, p. 32). These three features have been vital in the establishment and growth of the capitalist world-system; they are at the root of all significant capital accumulation. However, the very success of this system,

Wallerstein asserts, has undermined these foundations and must necessarily lead to its decline and fall.

Like Marx before him, Wallerstein predicts that internal contradictions within capitalism will eventually bring about the fall of the system. He sees these contradictions as already producing serious dysfunctions throughout the globe; consequently, he predicts, the fall will happen over the next twenty-five to fifty years. There are four interrelated, long-standing contradictions that, as they work themselves out, will eventually bring about the downfall of world capitalism and ultimately transform human social life.

The first contradiction is that capitalism depends on a significant portion of the world labor market that it can exploit through long working hours and low pay. The cost of labor, Wallerstein reports, is set through both supply and demand and the political power of both capitalists and workers (Wallerstein, 1999, p. 79). In the past, capitalists have met the demands of workers in the core states by drawing new workers from rural areas to offset these high wages and bring down the overall costs of production. Paying a portion of workers higher wages and benefits had the added function of creating consumers with the resources to purchase many of the products that the system produced. However, because of its very success in expanding throughout the world, capitalism is rapidly losing the easily exploitable portion of its labor market (Wallerstein, 1999, pp. 30–31). More and more people in peripheral areas (as well as in the core) are moving to urban centers in which worker concentration leads to greater bargaining power and higher expectations of a living wage and other benefits (Wallerstein, 1999, p. 31). This "deruralization" leads to increasing labor costs and thus must necessarily cut into the long-term accumulation of capital.

The second internal contradiction that runs counter to the accumulation of capital is caused by the "ecological crisis." Wallerstein believes there has been serious ecological degradation over the course of capitalist development, this despite the significant scientific and technical advances over the course of the centuries (Wallerstein, 1999, p. 76). Like other issues, positions vary on the degree of seriousness of the ecological crisis. Many see relatively easy technological solutions to the problems, others see doomsday. Wallerstein takes a moderate position, believing the crisis will necessitate some serious adjustment of the system. His focus here is not on the ecological consequences of the crisis, however, but how it affects the political economy of the world-system (Wallerstein, 1999, p. 76).

The culture of the capitalist world-system, Wallerstein points out, is defined by its emphasis on endless capital accumulation and growth, with little stress placed on any countervailing constraints. The very institutions of the world-system were constructed around these values (Wallerstein, 1999, p. 78). This view owes much to Weber's concept of rationalization, or the increasing dominance of formal rationality. Historical capitalism, Wallerstein asserts, made the endless accumulation of capital and all of its ideological justifications the primary organizing principle of the system. No other value is allowed to seriously check or soften this imperative. It is not that the values of capitalism are not found in previous civilizations, it is that in the present world-system they are virtually unchecked by any countervailing forces. "What we mean by historical capitalism is a system in which the institutions that were constructed made it possible for capitalist values to take priority, such that the world-economy was set upon the path of the commodification of everything in order that there be ceaseless accumulation of capital for its own sake" (Wallerstein, 1999, p. 78).

The extent of the environmental crisis is therefore directly attributable to the capitalist world-economy. Again, this is because of its very success—it has expanded production and thus population at a dramatic rate, and it has expanded all over the earth (Wallerstein, 1999, p. 82). Companies that depleted the environment or that polluted air, water, and land through their production processes were able to minimize their costs by ignoring the environmental havoc they created, leaving governments to bear the clean-up costs, thus spreading the costs to the population as a whole.[17] The fact that companies could externalize these costs means that there is no incentive to factor ecology into corporate decisions (Wallerstein, 1999, p. 85).

And the ecological crisis must necessarily intensify. Companies are expanding their markets; more people around the globe are demanding entrance into consumer culture, population is still expanding (Wallerstein, 1999, p. 79). As the crisis intensifies the budgets of national governments are increasingly stretched to provide for the cleanup. This, predicts Wallerstein, will cause governments to try to force companies to internalize these costs, which will cut deeply into their capital accumulation (Wallerstein, 1999, p. 31). These steps, Wallerstein believes, will prove costly and must seriously erode capital accumulation (Wallerstein, 1999, p. 81).

It is not the case that the increased costs for labor and for environmental clean-up can be merely passed on to consumers in the form of higher prices. Profit on a product, Wallerstein explains, is the difference of the sales price minus the cost of production multiplied by the number of sales. "That is to say, the 'market' constrains the sales price, in that, at a certain point, the price becomes so high that the total sales profit is less than if the sales price were lower" (Wallerstein, 1999, p. 79). Factoring in increased costs for labor and for ecology will seriously squeeze profit margins, which must seriously erode the ability of the system to accumulate capital (Wallerstein, 1999, p. 80).

The third trend that is hindering the continued operation of the capitalist world-system is the spread of democracy around the world. Wallerstein sees this spread as both real and significant for the political economy of the world-system. The spread of democracy brings the demands of the masses for decent jobs, medical care, education, consumer goods, and housing more directly into the political calculations of the state (Wallerstein, 2000, pp. 385–386). In the beginning the demands for a living wage, welfare, health care, education, and other social amenities were confined to the core states (mainly Europe and North America) and could be met with modest expenditures. "Today, workers everywhere expect it, and the level of their demands is significantly higher than it was even fifty years ago. Ultimately, these moneys can only come at the cost of accumulating capital" (Wallerstein, 1999, pp. 31–32). The demands for income, health care and education, in particular, seem to be insatiable.

> To the extent that there is democratization, people insist not merely on having these three, but on regularly raising the minimal threshold for each. But having these three, at the level that people are demanding each day, is incredibly expensive, even for the wealthy countries, not to speak of Russia, China, and India. The only way everyone can really have more of these is to have a radically different system of distribution of the world's resources than we have today. (Wallerstein, 2000, p. 386)

The fourth internal contradiction that is weakening the accumulation of capital is the decline in the power of the state. Wallerstein points out that the power of the nation-state had been increasing in the world since the establishment of the capitalist world-system, but that this trend has recently been reversed (Wallerstein, 1999, p. 32). State power has been critical for capitalism, serving to keep internal order, sponsoring national and international monopolies, and taking other steps to promote and protect the accumulation of capital. The state creates monopolies and supports profits through purchasing, trade, and tax policies (Wallerstein, 1999, p. 65). It directly assumes some of the costs of production by building infrastructure (roads, sewers, and such) and indirectly through environmental policies (Wallerstein, 1999, p. 63). In addition, the nation-state restrains labor unions through labor laws as well as moves to "soften discontent" of the "dangerous classes" through the expansion of the welfare state (Wallerstein, 1999, p. 74).

Why is state power declining? The primary reason, according to Wallerstein, is that their populations are losing faith in them; they are rapidly losing legitimacy (Wallerstein, 1999, pp. 74–75). This loss of faith, Wallerstein believes, is rooted in the realization that liberal reform of the system simply cannot address its failures. Extreme poverty within states, the north-south polarization between states, ecological depletion and pollution, and the failure of even antisystemic movements to seriously address these problems has led to the loss of faith in inevitable progress through state action.

Liberalism, Wallerstein argues, is the ideology of the capitalist class constructed to mollify the "dangerous classes" since the time of the French Revolution (Wallerstein, 2000, p. 428). To the insistent demands of the dangerous classes for immediate redistribution of national resources, liberal reform promised material progress—the gradual redistribution of the growing surplus to address inequalities. Liberalism became the dominant ideology of elites throughout the nineteenth and most of the twentieth century, even subtly changing (and thus undermining) radical-socialism and conservative ideology with its promises of reform and inevitable progress. Disillusionment set in after World War II as reformist regimes took over governments throughout the world and failed to deliver. World-wide faith in liberalism and the promise of reform came crashing down, Wallerstein asserts, with the widespread social revolutions of 1968, culminating in the collapse of communism in 1989 (Wallerstein, 2000, p. 428).

But state power is essential for the accumulation of capital, essential for the continued operation of the capitalist world-system (Wallerstein, 1999, pp. 74–75). Precisely at the time when corporations are feeling the profit squeeze caused by higher labor costs they are being pressured to internalize more of the costs of production, and to give up more of their capital for national redistribution. In addition, nation-states are under pressure to eliminate direct subsidies to corporations, a significant source of capital accumulation (Wallerstein, 1999, pp. 80–81). The struggle will intensify in the coming years, particularly over environmental issues—they will be at the forefront of the debate because the externalization of costs remains one of the most significant sources of capital (Wallerstein, 1999, p. 85). But the system is in terminal crisis, Wallerstein argues, because all of the avenues of significant capital accumulation are being narrowed; capital accumulation no longer has free reign, nor can the state easily lift the restrictions.

We are now in a period of transition; the next twenty-five to fifty years will be a period of struggle in which the new system (or systems) will be born. Wallerstein predicts that we will see escalating local and regional violence, as well as nuclear, biological, and chemical weapons proliferation (Wallerstein, 2000, p. 384). The end of the Cold War, and the decline of American hegemony, Wallerstein has long claimed, has led to a certain amount of instability in the world.

Another factor that will add to world unrest is the increasing rate of migration from peripheral and semi-peripheral regions to core countries. This includes the south–north migration as well as the eastern-Europe to western-Europe migration. These rates of migration are growing, Wallerstein asserts, because of the labor needs of capitalist enterprises in core states, improvements in transportation, the increasing economic and demographic polarization between core and periphery,[18] and because of the spread of democratic ideology. This ideology, he says, makes it more politically difficult for the wealthy states to control their borders (Wallerstein, 2000, p. 384).

Increased rates of migration will contribute to disorder in several ways. This would include right-wing movements to restrict the flow of immigration, greater legal and physical barriers at the borders, and increasing friction between races and ethnic groups (Wallerstein, 2000, p. 384–385). But the forces causing the increased migration will not easily be turned, Wallerstein predicts, the rates will continue to grow. This immigration will lead to the establishment of an increasingly significant racial/ethnic underclass in all core states. It is likely that they will not be easily assimilated; that they will be discriminated against and exploited (Wallerstein, 2000, p. 385). Wallerstein adds that this underclass will be without the faith in progress of previous generations, a faith that served to justify much inequality with the knowledge that hard work would produce a better world for you and your children (Wallerstein, 2000, p. 385).

Also contributing to the world disorders, Wallerstein submits, are the increasing urbanization, rising levels of education, and improved communications which promotes political awareness and mobilization. This makes it ever more "difficult to obscure the degree of disparities and the role of governments in maintaining them" (Wallerstein, 2000, p. 430).[19] Yet another factor contributing to the disorder is the fiscal crisis of governments caused by the increased costs of subsidies to capitalism and expansion of the welfare state while at the same time being constrained by tax revolts and a loss of faith among the citizenry. The battle between newly aware citizens and corporations over the state's resources will be the focus of class struggle (Wallerstein, 2000, p. 430).

As the disorder mounts, Wallerstein expects that the world-system will continue to operate as it has done in the past. "Capitalists will seek support from state structures as they have in the past. States will compete with other states to be the major loci of the accumulation of capital" (Wallerstein, 2000, p. 431). The system will continue to expand, more and more activities will be commodified, populations will become further polarized in terms of wealth and power. But the states will gradually loose legitimacy and find it increasingly difficult to maintain order both internally or internationally. An increasingly wealthy North will confront an increasingly exploited and desperate South, but one with increasing military power (Wallerstein, 2000, pp. 414–415). Because of its slipping economic status, as well as the proliferation of weapons of mass destruction, the United States will no longer be the hegemonic power that has so dominated and ordered the world in the latter half of the twentieth century. The capitalist world-system will slip into chaos and a new order will eventually emerge (Wallerstein, 2000, p. 431).

Unlike Marx, Wallerstein does not predict precisely what this new world order will be. There is no inevitability of something better or worse. What emerges very much depends upon the ongoing struggle. The major fault of the capitalist world-system, Wallerstein believes, is that it has been totally constructed around the ever-greater accumulation of capital. Until recently, it has effectively minimized forces that attempt to impose constraints on this accumulation (Wallerstein, 1999, p. 82). As a result, it has created unprecedented wealth for a substantial number of the world's population (Wallerstein estimates as much as one-seventh to one-fifth of the world's population) and great poverty for everyone else (Wallerstein, 2000, p. 432). While other systems have had similar inequalities, Wallerstein asserts, no other allowed a substantial minority to live so well while the bulk lived so poorly. As a result of the struggle, the world-system will either move toward a repressive or an egalitarian restructuring (Wallerstein, 2000, p. 413).

Progressive forces will push for an egalitarian distribution of resources and thus necessarily, a democratic distribution of power (Wallerstein, 1999, p. 3). It is at this point that Wallerstein's conception of the social sciences again comes into play. We should be on the side of these progressive forces. We should be investigating alternative social systems that are possible, weighing their strengths and weaknesses. Invoking Weber's concept of "substantive rationality," he asserts that all social decisions must be made in a context of competing values and different group interests. "It presumes that there is never any system that can realize fully all these sets of values simultaneously, even if we were to feel that each set of values is meritorious. To be substantively rational is to make choices that will provide an optimal mix" (Wallerstein, 1999, p. 85). We must be on the side of those people whose aim is building a system in which social decisions are made collectively, where real alternatives are debated. We must do all we can to bring about a system in which decisions of production and consumption are rooted in broader social values of sustainability, beauty, and community, not simply in the accumulation of more capital (Wallerstein, 1999, p. 86). We must be on the side of progressive forces in this struggle—to practice social science as a value-neutral exercise in formal rationality is destructive to the human community (Wallerstein, 2000, pp. 433–434).

EXCURSUS: DECLINING PROFITS AND HEGEMONY?

Wallerstein argues that the recent globalization arguments of social scientists usually miss the fact that capitalism has depended upon a world-wide division of labor for production and marketing goods from the beginning. This may be so, but the increase in trade in the latter half of the twentieth century has still been remarkable. Table 3.1 illustrates the growth of American trade as a percentage of the American Gross Domestic Product (GDP) for selected years from 1960 to 2000. As illustrated, the dollar value of imports and exports as a percentage of GDP climbed from 9 percent in 1960 to 26 percent in 2000. Part of this

Table 3.1: Trade as a percent of GDP (actual dollars)

	Exports	Imports	Total	GDP	Percent
1960	25,940	22,432	48,372	526.4	9%
1970	56,640	54,386	111,026	1,038	11%
1980	271,834	291,241	563,075	2,789	20%
1990	535,233	616,093	1,151,326	5,803	20%
2000	1,070,054	1,445,438	2,515,492	9,817	26%

Sources: GDP: Economic History Service http://eh.net/hmit/gdp/ Trade: U.S. Census Bureau, Foreign Trade Division

increase, particularly the rise in the dollar value of imports, is undoubt-
edly the result of the gradual erosion of American hegemony. Increasingly, American companies had to compete for their own domestic
markets. Initially in the 1970s and 80s, the old-line oligopolies had
trouble holding on to their market shares. In the 1950s and 60s Japan
and Western European capitalists were building new plants using the
latest in technology and disciplined/organized work forces, while
American corporations were taking huge profits, and enlarging their
bureaucracies. European and Japanese markets were often highly competitive internally, the best then receiving government subsidies to con-
quer new markets abroad. Now, China, Korea, and other Pacific Rim
nations are competing as well. American corporations were in choreographed competition with each other from the end of WWII to the early
1980s, most being satisfied to maintain their market share. Now they
must compete fiercely with the enterprises of other nations.

Wallerstein's prediction of the decline and fall of capitalism relies
heavily on declining profits as a result of increasing labor costs, the
weakening of state power on their behalf, and increasing internalization
of environmental costs associated with production. To this point, however, U.S. corporations appear to be countering these increased costs
through several strategies. Like their world competitors, American corporations have used robots, automation, and computer and communications technologies to downsize their workforce, turned more frequently
to contingency workers; outsourced manufacturing jobs to periphery
and semiperiphery areas; and tightened the coordination, manipulation
and the wages of the permanent workforce that has remained. Table 3.2
shows that this strategy has been successful in maintaining and even
increasing profit margins. The table displays an average of Total U.S.
Corporate Profits (after taxes) for each decade since World War II. As
shown, total U.S. corporate profits, which include all domestic and foreign affiliates of U.S. corporations, averaged $24.9 billion in the 1950s,
climbing rapidly to an average of over $372 billion in the 1990s. In
fact, average corporate profits in the 1990s were two times the average
profits of the 1980s, three times the average of the 1970s, and eight
times the average of the 1960s.

Table 3.2: Average Annual U.S. Corporate Profits by Decade: 1950 to
2000

	50-59	60-69	70-79	80-89	90-99
Average Corporate Profits (millions)	24,948	42,384	120,002	157,937	372,242
% From Foreign Investment[20]	9	11	16	24	23

Source: U.S. Department of Commerce, Bureau of Economic Analysis

Also displayed in this table is the average annual percentage of total corporate profits generated overseas. As can be seen, this percentage averages 9 percent through the 1950s and 11 percent in the 60s. In the 1970s this percentage begins to climb rapidly, reaching about 23 percent through the 80s and 90s. This is not a measure of trade; rather it represents the percentage of total profit made by American corporations (and individuals) in investments overseas. For example, in 1998 total corporate profits were $469.9 billion. Of this total, $102.9 billion, or 22 percent of the total U.S. corporate profit for that year, was taken from foreign investments, more than any single domestic industry.

Table 3.3 displays the after-tax domestic profit for U.S. corporations averaged by decade. It also shows the percentage contribution for selected industries. As can be seen, total domestic profit by U.S. corporations averaged $22.7 billion annually in the 1950s. In that decade "Manufacturing" accounted for 53 percent of all domestic profits; "Finance" accounted for 16 percent, "Services" for only about 2 percent. The slide in the percentage of profits taken from domestic manufacturing begins to take place in the 70s and 80s, and becomes quite pronounced in the 90s, falling to just 26 percent of the domestic industry total. Does this mean that manufacturing is no longer profitable in the U.S.? No, total domestic profits for manufacturing averaged about $50 billion a year in the U.S. in the 1980s, but more than $82 billion a year in the 1990s, a growth of some 64 percent. Profits in U.S. manufacturing are strong and still growing; manufacturing still is the most profitable of all domestic industries. However, the profits of other industries are presently growing at a much faster rate than that of manufacturing.

Table 3.3: Profits of U.S. Industry Averaged by Decade

	50-59	60-69	70-79	80-89	90-99
Domestic Corporate Profits (millions)	22,731	37,883	86,909	132,662	317,680
Domestic Industries Percent:					
Construction	1.6	2	3	4	5
Manufacturing	53	50	44	38	26
Wholesale trade	5	6	12	13	8
Retail trade	7	8	9	10	11
Finance, insurance, and real estate	13	16	16	12	25
Services	1.5	2	3	7	9
All others	16	16	13	16	16

Source: Computed from profit data gathered by the Bureau of Economic Analysis, U.S. Department of Commerce.

Recall that Wallerstein posited that hegemonic powers gain ascendancy first through dominance in agricultural and manufacturing productivity, then in commerce, and then in finance; and lose this ascendancy in this order as well. Consistent with this "financialization" hypotheses, finance and insurance are well on their way to becoming the dominant sector in the American economy. The "Finance, insurance and real estate" industry accounted for a full 25 percent of all domestic profits in the 90s, almost equal to that of manufacturing. A breakdown of this growth provided by the Bureau of Economic Analysis reveals that the increase is made up almost entirely of growth in the profits of "Depository institutions" and "Commercial and mutual depository institutions" beginning in 1990 and rising rapidly throughout the decade. This was probably the result of federal deregulation of the banking and savings and loan industries, and the investment of deposits into a rapidly growing economy (recall, the GDP, which was large already in 1987, doubled in just 14 years). The profitability of the two types of depository institutions combined rose from $53.6 billion in 1987 to $141.6 billion in 1999. With the passage of "The Financial Services Modernization Act of 1999" growth in profitability of banking will accelerate (Dye, 2002, p. 43).[21]

Other industries that increased their profitability in the 1990s, though not so rapidly, were "Services," which went from 3 percent of all profits in the 70s to 9 percent in the 90s, and Construction, which climbed to 5 percent of all domestic profit. The growth in services in large part appears to be due to changes in the delivery of health services, which climbed from $4.8 billion in profits in 1987 to $16 billion in 1999. In the 1970s and 80s medicine was more likely to be practiced by private practitioner physicians, hospital care provided through government or charitable hospitals. Since the 1980s the U.S. has seen a sharp rise in corporate medicine, which gives medicine tremendous impetus for growth, innovation, and the efficient delivery of services (at least those services which are potentially profitable), but which, in Harry Braverman's (1974) memorable phrase, must pay tribute to profit. A second service category that grew rapidly in the 1990s is "Other" services, which consists of engineering and management services, membership organizations, and for-profit social services. This category begins at $1.5 billion in profits in 1987 and rises to $9.3 billion in profits by 1999.

Such is the growth of capital in the United States in the latter half of the twentieth century. It is this drive for increasing profit on the part of corporations and individuals that fuels the vigorous growth of industries. What then are these profits used for? Some capital, of course, is used to pay dividends to the stockholders of the corporation. Individual stockholders siphon off some portion for living expenses, comforts, and displays of status and reinvest the rest in economic enterprises in order to increase their capital. Corporations also use their profits to expand their core business, hiring new employees, purchasing new technologies, further refining the detailed division of labor, all with an eye toward increasing profitability. Should the corporation see larger profit opportunities elsewhere, it will decide to invest in plants or businesses overseas, start new enterprises at home, or buy out other businesses that could ultimately increase the organization's profit potential.

The major function of capitalism, then, is to expand capital. It does this by increasing economic activity. This expansion, in turn, increases employment, wealth, and ultimately, population. This then expands capital even further. It is, as both admirers and detractors have all remarked, quite a dynamic engine. For any macrosocial theory or analysis to ignore the operations and functions of this engine in the modern world—or to fail to take into account the structure, functions, and interests of the capitalist world-system—is to engage in empty academic exercise.

ABOUT WALLERSTEIN

Immanuel Wallerstein was born September 8, 1930, in New York City. He reports that he was politically conscious from a very early age, apparently picking up socialist politics from his family in the early 1940s. While the primary political concern of his family was the defeat of fascism at this time, Immanuel was also torn by the split between the Second and Third Internationals (social democrats and communists). Immanuel found Stalin era communists unprincipled, opportunistic, autocratic, and evil. But he found the social democrats of the day to be weak on issues of inequality and race, as well as being far too willing to compromise or give in to nationalist tendencies (Wallerstein, 2000, p. xv). Eventually, Wallerstein comes to see this split in the opposition to capitalism (or what he has come to term "anti-systemic movements") as due to "systemic constraints" imposed by the capitalist system itself (Wallerstein, 2000, pp. xv–xvi).

Wallerstein entered Columbia College in 1947 and continued his passion for politics. Graduating Columbia with a BA in 1951, he served in the U.S. Army from 1951–53, and returned to Columbia to complete a master's thesis on McCarthyism in 1954. "I drew on Wright Mills's distinction in *New Men of Labor* between sophisticated conservatives and the practical right, to argue that McCarthyism was a program of the practical right, only marginally concerned with Communists and in fact directed primarily against the sophisticated conservatives" (Wallerstein, 2000, p. xvi). He began to specialize in political sociology.

As a political sociologist he made Africa his initial specialty, this at a time when Africa was dominated by colonial powers but struggling for independence. He received a Ford Foundation African Fellowship to study and write his dissertation on the role of voluntary associations in the rise of nationalist movements in the Gold Coast and the Ivory Coast (Wallerstein, 2000, p. xvi). Wallerstein went on to complete his Ph.D. degree from Columbia[22] in 1959. "If my intellectual quest led me early on away from the familiar grounds of my own country to contemporary Africa ... it was because I had a gut feeling in the 1950s that the most important thing happening in the twentieth century was the struggle to overcome the control of the West of the rest of the world" (Wallerstein, 2000, pp. xvi–xvii). So, while his fellow social scientists considered the Cold War struggle between communism and capitalism, or totalitarianism and democracy, to be the central defining issue of the time, Wallerstein had early on focused on the struggle between core and periphery, "the fundamental and ongoing polarization of the capitalist world-economy (Wallerstein, 2000, p. xxii).

Over the next twenty years his views evolved until by the early 1970s, he reports, he had developed a perspective that he called "world-systems analysis." This involved two interrelated "intellectual decisions." First, you could only fully comprehend social reality through a complete unit of analysis, and this has to be at the world-system level. And second, social analysis must be simultaneously historic (idiographic humanism) and systemic (nomothetic science) (Wallerstein, 2000, p. xvii).

In addition to his exposure to the great debates between the Second and Third Internationals in his formative years and his immersion in the African liberation movements of the 1950s and 1960s, Wallerstein identifies one additional "turning point" in his intellectual development. This was "world revolution of 1968, which I experienced directly at Columbia University, and which helped expunge from my thinking both the lingering illusions of liberalism and a rosy view of the antisystemic movements. It sobered me up" (Wallerstein, 2000, p. xxii).

Wallerstein served in the Department of Sociology at Columbia from 1958 to 1971, and then went on to McGill University (1971–1976), SUNY at Binghamton (1976–1999), and is currently at Yale University. Wallerstein has also been the director of the Fernand

Braudel Center for the Study of Economics, Historical Systems, and Civilizations since 1976. He has received many awards and honors over his long and distinguished career. These include the Career of Distinguished Scholarship Award from the American Sociological Association (2003), as well as being a Fellow in the American Academy of Sciences.

NOTES

1. The first watershed is, of course, the Neolithic or agricultural revolution. Much studied by anthropologists, a description of the process of the domestication of plants and animals is contained in the chapter on Harris.

2. It is widely believed (and Wallerstein notes) that patterning the social sciences after the natural sciences, was an attempt to not only borrow successful empirical methods but also the resulting prestige of natural science.

3. The continued dominance of the idiographic method in Anthropology may go a long way toward the seeming affinity of this discipline and postmodernism.

4. That is, one that will further our understanding of the world.

5. "Corporate structures" is the term used by Wallerstein.

6. Mills points out that the bureaucratic needs for social research provides for a lot of employment.

7. For Wallerstein, it is the competition and conflict among and between these groups that dominates. Consensus and cooperation leading to equilibrium are ephemeral; conflict—sometimes institutionalized, sometimes openly violent—is much more the norm (2000, p. xix).

8. Having authored a book titled *The Evolution of the Future* that had a similar theme, I am rather fond of this quote,

9. "Substantive rationality" is Weber's term that refers to rational thought and action in a holistic context of enduring human values. A more contemporary term (but perhaps more meaningless because it has attained the status of a buzz word) might well be "critical thinking."

10. Unlike traditional Marxists, Wallerstein does not assume that all labor in the capitalist world-system must ultimately be based on wages or that capitalism can only exist in an industrial economy (2000, p. 85). Wallerstein recognizes that capitalist labor can take many forms—for example, slavery, serfdom, sharecropping (2000, pp. 78–79). He also recognizes that "agricultural capitalism" preceded the industrial revolution (1974, pp. 350–351). The major characteristics of capitalism, according to Wallerstein, are the production of goods or services for sale in a market for profit (2000, pp. 84–85) and the ceaseless accumulation of capital (1999, p. 78).

11. "What we mean by a liberal state is one in which the amount of force is reduced and the amount of deception and concessions increased" (1999, p. 66).

12. Or between North and South, or First and Third World.

13. This, Wallerstein adds, is neither utopian nor imminent; but it is a possible outcome of struggle.

14. International relations at the two ends of the continuum, Wallerstein adds, are both rare and unstable; more normal times—or the middle of the continuum—have the various nation states allied in two groups with a rough balance of power between them. In this situation, no single nation, or group of nations, can long dominate.

15. This is 1914 to 1945 for the United States Wallerstein (and many others) interpret the Second World War as a continuation of the First, a struggle essentially between Germany and the United States for dominance or hegemony in the world-system.

16. Wallerstein adds that this should not be perceived as a catastrophe. The United States will not become some backwater, it just will not dominate economically, militarily, culturally, and politically as it has in the latter half of the twentieth century (2000, p. 409). All things must pass.

17. The profits, of course, go to the company.

18. The rich are getting richer and the poor are getting babies.

19. It is curious but Wallerstein never adequately addresses the reverse hypothesis, that improved communications, rising levels of education (educated people have to have an opinion and may more readily take one ready-made), and urbanization, lead to improved levers of manipulation and control. The success of recent American governments pursuing policies clearly in the interests of the corporate structure against the interests of both the dangerous classes as well as the middle classes—this while securing their votes—would seem to be a strong argument that these new levers of power are powerful indeed. Beginning with Reagan, each succeeding administration (with the possible exception of Bush Senior) seems to be more media savvy, more effective at manipulating both media and public opinion.

20. Consists of receipts by all U.S. residents, including both corporations and persons; of dividends from foreign corporations; and for U.S. corporations, their share of reinvested earnings of their incorporated foreign affiliates; and earnings of unincorporated foreign affiliates, net of corresponding payments.

21. Following Wallerstein, Kevin Phillips also argues that this financialization of the economy is the mark of a hegemonic power in decline.

22. Each of the theorists covered to this point have a strong connection to Columbia—a hotbed of macrolevel theory?

4

Gerhard Lenski's Ecological-Evolutionary Theory

Evolutionary perspectives in sociology had largely fallen into disuse since the nineteenth century. Until relatively recently, they were subject to rejection out-of-hand, even ridicule, by major figures in the field (Lenski, 2005, p. 3). In an effort to attract students, sociology concentrated more on social-psychology; in an effort to attract research dollars, the field focused on theories of the "middle-range," simple relationships between social phenomena and human behavior rather than the all-encompassing systems of the founders. Sociological theory in general has become the arcane specialty of a few, with its own vocabulary, limited readership, and even more limited applications.

Gerhard Lenski was one of the first to go against this trend in sociology. Since the mid-1960s Lenski has been developing an ecological-evolutionary theory that is broad in scope and capable of synthesizing many of the insights and findings of the discipline into a coherent framework; capable of furthering our understanding of sociocultural systems as a whole. Through his work Lenski constructs an ecological-evolutionary theory, synthesizing classical and contemporary theory in the social sciences (sociology, archaeology, history, political science, and economics) and biology into a comprehensive theory of social evolution (Lenski, 2005, pp. xiv–xv). In the classical tradition of the nineteenth century he has constructed a holistic theory of sociocultural systems, a theory that has proven itself to be powerful, testable, and capable of providing new insights in our attempts to understand sociocultural stability and change. Through successive editions of a major introductory text, he attempts to explain to undergraduates the origin, stability, and evolution of societies through time.[1]

Also like the nineteenth century theorists, his method is both deductive and inductive. Taking elements of classical theories as his starting point, he then examines empirical findings (ethnographies, histories, and comparative sociological studies) and modifies his theory accordingly. It is this method which undergirds his book on the causes of inequality in sociocultural systems, *Power and Privilege* (1966). It is the same method he uses to develop his more general ecological-evolutionary theory in a succession of eight editions of *Human Societies* (this book is now in its ninth edition, but Lenski is no longer the lead author) and more recently in *Ecological-Evolutionary Theory* (2005). In this manner, Lenski synthesized his theory, tested it against the evidence, and refined it in a continuous process from the mid-1960s to 2005. Lenski is a strong advocate of both inductive and deductive logic in building social theory. Because of the complexity of social systems, he believes, the scholar must constantly shift back and forth between theory and the data, continuously testing theoretical hypotheses which—depending upon the evidence—leads to refinement and further tests of the theory (Lenski, 2005, p. 14). While he begins from basic premises and assumptions, he modifies these assumptions and adds refinements and additional generalizations as empirical evidence dictates. His method thus allows for an interaction between deductive and inductive reasoning (Lenski, 1966, pp. 23–24). Figure 4.1 illustrates this model of theory building.

The deductive part of Lenski's theory begins from the insights of T. Robert Malthus, an economist and demographer of the early nineteenth century. From Malthus Lenski borrows the observation that human societies are part of the world of nature. Human societies are subject to natural law. Sociocultural systems can only be fully understood as being responsive to the interactions of populations to their environments (Lenski and Lenski, 1987, p. 55).

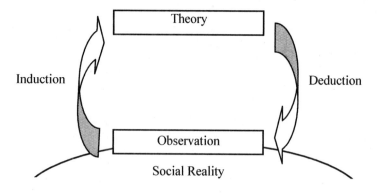

Figure 4.1: Induction and Deduction in Theory Building

Like Malthus's theory, at the base of Lenski's perspective lies the relationship between population and production. Like all life forms humans have a reproductive capacity that substantially exceeds the necessary subsistence resources in the environment. Thus, Lenski concludes, human populations tend to grow until they come up against the limits of food production, and then they are checked (Lenski and Lenski, 1987, p. 32; Lenski, 2005, p. 57). The checks, of course, consist of both the positive and preventive checks that Malthus first explored in 1798. The capacity for population growth, Lenski asserts, has been a "profoundly destabilizing force throughout human history and may well be the ultimate source of most social and cultural change" (Lenski & Lenski, 1987, p. 32). Lenski posits that the relationships among population, production, and environment drive the evolution of sociocultural systems.

The influence of Malthus is also clearly apparent when Lenski discusses the nature of social inequality. Like Malthus, he asserts that we are social animals obliged to cooperate with one another in producing a living (Lenski, 1966, p. 24; 2005, p. 37). Also like Malthus, he claims that human beings are strongly motivated by self-interest. Lenski believes that this self-interest is rooted in our species' genetic heritage. Because our behavior and attitude formation is so dependent upon learning and individual experience—and because no two humans can possibly be exposed to the identical learning/experiential process—human beings develop differences and a sense of individual identity. These quickly lead to the formation of self-interest (Lenski, 2005, pp. 37–38). Therefore, Lenski states *"when men are confronted with important decisions where they are obliged to choose between their own, or their group's, interests and the interests of others, they nearly always choose the former*—though often seeking to hide this fact from themselves and others" (Lenski, 1966, p. 30, emphasis in the original).

Since most necessary resources are in short supply, he continues, a struggle for rewards will be present in every human society. Individuals are born with a range of innate abilities and circumstances. Thus the root of social inequality is in our nature. Some minimal distribution of wealth is necessary to ensure the survival of "others whose actions are necessary" to themselves, but any surplus (goods and services over and above the minimum required to keep necessary workers alive and productive) will be distributed unequally (Lenski, 1966, pp. 44–45).

In the earlier stages of sociocultural evolution the distribution of resources is allocated on the basis of personal characteristics—hunting skills or plant-gathering productivity. With the development of a more complex division of labor these inequalities become institutionalized in class, caste, race, sex, and ethnic systems. Thus, like Malthus before him, Lenski concludes that inequality is inevitable in any complex so-ciocultural system (complex as measured by a division of labor), though the degree of inequality is variable across societies and through time (Lenski, 1966, p. 442).

While it begins with Malthus, Lenski's perspective is an integrat-ing device as well. By his own report, his other major theoretical influ-ences have been Herbert Spencer, Charles Darwin, Karl Marx, Fried-rich Engels, Max Weber, Robert Michels, and Thorstein Veblen. More contemporary influences include C. Wright Mills, Leslie White, and Marvin Harris (Lenski, Lenski and Nolan, 1991, p. xviii; Lenski, 2005, p. 11). One can see the influence of Weber in Lenski's discussion of power and the multidimensional nature of stratification; the influence of Veblen as Lenski writes on the importance of status and status striv-ing; the influence of Mills as Lenski discusses power, authority, and manipulation; and the influence of White on Lenski's discussion of the importance of technological change. Finally, one can certainly see the influence of Harris in Lenski's growing focus in later editions of *Hu-man Societies* on the centrality of environmental, technological, and population variables, as well as the importance of feedback from social structures and cultural superstructures in determining the direction of sociocultural change.

SOCIAL EVOLUTION

Like evolutionary theory in biology, Lenski puts forward ecological-evolutionary social theory as an all-encompassing paradigm for sociol-ogy that can serve as a viable framework to bring order and research focus to the discipline. But should the social sciences even be using the term evolution? Stephen J. Gould was a professor of zoology and geol-ogy and one of the most vigorous defenders and popular teachers of natural evolution in the last half of the twentieth century. For most of his professional life he struggled against the idea of "progress" in natu-ral evolution, both in the popular mind as well as a distorting image among some of his professional colleagues. In several of his essays Gould (1992, 1996) decries the use of the term "cultural evolution" because the process is so very different from natural selection in nature.

Gould (1992) identifies three major differences between natural evolution and social evolution (what Gould prefers to call simply social change):

First, cultural evolution does not rely on inherited characteristics; rather its chief mechanism of descent is learning. Successful innovations can be directly taught to the next generation.

Second, genetic change takes place over generations, sociocultural change can occur within a matter of months or even days. Biological evolution is indirect, relying upon fortuitous genetic variation that will enable the organism to adapt to a changing environment; sociocultural adaptation to changing natural and social environments is far more direct and potentially purposeful.

Finally, and most distressing to Gould, biological evolution is a system of divergence. Once a species becomes separate, it cannot recombine, it is separate forever. Yet in sociocultural evolution "transmission across lineages" (cultural transmission) is probably the chief avenue of change. (Gould, 1992, p. 65)

In 1996 Gould added,

> Natural evolution includes no principle of predictable progress or movement to greater complexity. But cultural change is potentially progressive or 'self-complexifying' because Lamarckian inheritance [learned adaptation] accumulates favorable innovations by direct transmission, and amalgamation of traditions allows any culture to choose and join the most useful inventions of several separate societies. (p. 222)

Because of the different mechanisms of change (learning, cultural contact), and the sheer speed of change in sociocultural systems and the apparent directionality to sociocultural change (increasing complexity), Gould expresses the wish that social scientists would just use the more neutral term "cultural change" and stop confusing people.

Yet, as Gould knew full well, biology and the social sciences have always had a symbiotic relationship in terms of evolutionary theory. Both Darwin and Wallace (a cofounder of natural evolutionary theory) credited Malthus as a critical influence on the development of natural evolutionary theory. The term *evolution* itself was actually popularized by another social scientist and contemporary of Darwin's, Herbert Spencer. Darwin did not even use the term "evolution" in the first edition of *Origin of Species*, he preferred "descent with modifications" (Gould, 1996, p. 137).

It is important to keep in mind the differences as well as the parallels between natural and social evolution, for practitioners within biology as well as those in the social sciences. While drawing false parallels between growing complexity (sometimes simply labeled "progress") in sociocultural systems with natural systems, many biologists misled themselves and the general public into believing that life naturally progresses toward complexity. At the same time, social observers have been misled by faulty analogies between social and biological evolution as well. The misapplication of biological evolution by the "Social Darwinists," 19th century social scientists who characterized nature's struggle as bloody and brutish and used this faulty biological model to justify the inequality around them, still haunts social evolutionary theory today.

Lenski et al. (1991, pp. 66–68) acknowledge the same basic differences between natural and social evolution as those noted by Gould. But like Spencer before him, Lenski insists that sociocultural evolution is but a special case of the general evolutionary process.

> Viewed from the perspective of the new science of genetics, it is clear that far more than analogy is involved. Both sociocultural and organic evolution are processes by which populations have been formed and transformed in response to changes in the stores of heritable or transferable information they possess. In organic evolution, it is the entire population of living things, human and nonhuman alike, that have been formed and transformed; in sociocultural evolution, it is the human population alone. Thus, both organic and sociocultural evolution may be defined as the cumulation of heritable or transferable information within populations and its attendant consequences. (Lenski 2005, p. 43)

Human populations, Lenski points out, are subject to environmental and biological influences just as animal populations are. Rather than relying on genetic change to adapt to changes in the external environment, however, human populations have evolved culture. The process of evolution itself—inorganic-organic-social—is itself cumulative and evolving" (Lenski, 2005, p. 121). Lenski's ecological-evolutionary theory of sociocultural systems begins with and remains rooted in the basic biological paradigm.

One of the distinguishing characteristics of both biological and social evolution is the cumulative nature of change (Lenski, 2005, pp. 39–40). "Cumulative change," according to Lenski, "is a distinctive kind of change associated with systems composed of multiple, interrelated parts. Within these systems, some parts change while others remain unchanged. Thus, cumulative change is a process that combines elements of continuity with elements of change; many parts of the system are preserved for extended periods while new parts are added and other parts are either replaced or transformed (Lenski, 2005, p. 4). Earlier adaptations are "absorbed and incorporated" into newer biological or social systems, thus greatly influencing later adaptations. Just as an animal's past evolutionary history as well as its relation to the present environment is important in understanding that animal's adaptation to that environment, so too, a society's history or heritage is extremely important in understanding societal stability and change (Lenski, 2005, p. 188).

True to its subject matter and method of development, Lenski's theory itself has evolved over the years as Lenski examined more evidence and read more widely in the historical, anthropological, and sociological literature. *Power and Privilege* (1966) primarily presents an ecological theory of inequality. While the book examines a succession of societal types based on subsistence strategies, there is little theoretical development in explaining changes in these subsistence technologies. The various editions of *Human Societies* (1970–1995),[2] on the other hand, looks at both the relationships of sociocultural systems to their natural and social environments and evolutionary change both within and between societal types. *Ecological and Evolutionary Theory* (2005) is a summation of his life's work. In this chapter I will summarize Lenski's ecological-evolutionary theory using these three works as my primary sources. He begins, as most theorists do, by making a simple assertion about the nature of humans.

1. **Humans are by nature, social animals who engage in "antagonistic cooperation"(Lenski borrows this phrase from Sumner) in order to maximize their need satisfaction.**

Social life—cooperation with others—is necessary for both the survival of the species and for the "maximum satisfaction of human needs and desires" (Lenski, 1966, pp. 25–26). Human needs and desires include common basic physical needs across all human societies, such as the need for food, drink, sex, play, and personal survival. These basic physical needs are rooted in our genetic heritage (Lenski, 2005, p. 46). Humans seek to maximize pleasure and to minimize pain.

Also, since we are by nature social beings, the society into which we are born has a strong effect on shaping many of these basic needs and desires as well as creating "derivative" or secondary needs and desires (Lenski, 1966, p. 25–26; 2005, p. 47). In this list Lenski in-

cludes such drives as the need for love and affection, respect and prestige from our fellows, and for some type of meaning and order in life.
Since societies differ radically, the "nature and intensity" of these needs
vary *across* societies. Since individual experience within a particular
society differ radically, the "nature and intensity" of these needs vary
among individuals *within* the same society as well (Lenski et al., 1991,
p. 23).

Of all human needs and desires, Lenski notes, survival is given the
highest priority by the vast majority of human beings (Lenski, 1966, p.
37). This fact means that the threat of physical violence is a powerful
deterrent in human affairs. It also means that resources important for
survival (food and water and the resources needed to procure them) are
highly valued. Other widespread goals are health, prestige or social
honor, salvation, physical comfort, and love and affection. Still other
goals are sought, Lenski posits, because they help us attain these goals,
things such as money, office or position within an organization, or education and training (Lenski, 1966, pp. 37–40).

In addition to human needs and desires there are a variety of constants shared by humans across all human societies. Lenski notes that
humans everywhere have similar physiological and mental capabilities;
we have a great capacity for learning; for devising languages, symbol
systems and cultures (Lenski et al., 1991, pp. 23–25). These constants
serve as resources in striving to meet our primary and secondary needs.
In addition, Lenski adds, humans have a highly developed consciousness and a sense of the individual self; and we are often ruled by powerful emotions and appetites (Lenski et al., 1991, p. 25). These constants, Lenski makes clear, lead to the "antagonistic" character of social
life, for these two constants give humans strong motivation for putting
their own needs and desires ahead of others (Lenski et al., 1991, p. 26),
and are primarily responsible for the conflict and tension so characteristic in human societies (Lenski, 2000, pp. 38–39).

2. The resources needed by humans are in short supply. There-fore, a struggle for these resources is present in every society.

Like Malthus before him, Lenski notes that our reproductive capacity
exceeds our productive capacity. This is a normal feature of nature,
which scatters the seeds of life widely, but is comparatively miserly in
providing food and sustenance for this life. It is inevitable then, both
men remark, that many will die premature deaths, and others will live
close to the edge of starvation (Lenski, 1966, p. 31; Elwell, 2001, p.
136).

Lenski goes on to remark that, to "some extent" at any rate, humans have freed themselves from these constraints by learning to increase their food supply through cultivation, and control their reproduction through social practices and technologies (Lenski, 1966, p. 31). Malthus devoted a whole book (which also went through numerous editions) demonstrating that this "freedom" from nature's constraint was illusionary. Instead of freedom, Malthus insists, human populations must constantly adjust to the availability of resources through positive checks (shortening of lifespan) and preventive checks (social practices and birth control technology) on population growth. These continuous and necessary checks have profound impact on the rest of the sociocultural system. Lenski reaches the same conclusion in his later writings (see Lenski et al., 1991, p. 54 and throughout the book; Lenski, 2005, pp. 57–58). Population level and growth, along with subsistence technology, become prime causal agents in Lenski's general ecological-evolutionary theory.

Another point Lenski makes about the scarcity of goods and resources in his 1966 book is also relevant for other aspects of sociocultural systems and their impact on human behavior. Lenski asserts that humans appear to have an insatiable appetite for goods and services. "This is true chiefly because the goods and services have a status value as well as a utilitarian value" (Lenski, 1966, p. 31). Prestige or social honor, you will recall, is one of the chief needs or goals that Lenski identifies as universal. As a secondary or derivative goal, however, what goods and services bring social honor vary across societies and through time. What social actions are accorded high prestige and social honor also vary. Granting social honor (or scorn) is one of several ways society shapes the individual.

The struggle for resources within a sociocultural system is not necessarily violent. The struggle is often carried out within a system of economic and political rules. But even in the absence of violence, the struggle is serious for the men and women involved. Human beings are unequally endowed with physical abilities to compete in this struggle; though this is not the chief reason for the inequalities in human societies we see throughout history, it is a factor worthy of note (Lenski, 1966, pp. 31–32).

3.   **"Human societies are part of the global ecosystem and cannot be understood unless this fact is taken fully into account"**

Human societies are rooted in the environment, part of the world of nature (Lenski et al., 1991, pp. 6–8). As such, a society's environment has a profound influence on its social structure and culture. Lenski goes so far as to assert that all of a society's characteristics are ultimately due to just three things: the influence of the environment (both bio-physical and sociocultural), the influence of our species' genetic heri-tage, and the influence of prior sociocultural experience itself (Lenski et al., 1991, pp. 17–18; 2005, p. 76).

Sociocultural systems are the primary ways in which human beings adapt to their biological, physical, and social environments. A society's sociocultural environment consists of communications and contacts with other sociocultural systems. Adaptations to biophysical and so-ciocultural environments, Lenski asserts, are critical. The welfare of societal members as well as their very survival depends on how well their society adapts to these environments (Lenski et al., 1991, p. 10). As we will see, adaptation to changing biological, physical, and social environments is the engine of sociocultural evolution.

4. Society is an imperfect system that strives for stability and to meet the biological and psychological needs of its population.

Like most sociologists Lenski asserts that society is a system; however, he continues, it is an imperfect system at best (Lenski, 2005, p. 16). Analogies between societies and biological organisms or mechanical systems can be misleading, for such an analogy calls to mind perfect coordination and integration of the various parts of the system. This is not the case with sociocultural systems, in which the parts have varying degrees of autonomy and independence from the overall system (Len-ski, 1966, p. 34; Lenski et al., 1991, p. 20). The fact that society is an imperfect system means that not all of the parts function to strengthen the whole system. Many patterns and behaviors contribute nothing to the general welfare of the society, but rather serve the interests and needs of individuals or constituent groups. The fact that society is an imperfect system also means that conflict is a normal feature of all so-cieties, not an abnormal condition as posited by many functionalists (Lenski, 1966, p. 34). However, it is a sociocultural *system*, and as such there must be enough cooperation among the members of the society so that the system can maintain itself (Lenski et al., 1991, p. 21).[3]

Lenski asserts that societies have two basic goals (a) the mainte-nance of the political status quo within the society, and (b) the maximi-zation of production (Lenski, 1966, pp. 41–42). By maintenance of the political status quo Lenski means that societies strive to minimize po-litical change through laws and the machinery of state, police, military, and other agencies of social control. Societies also maintain themselves through fostering political ideologies that justify and celebrate the state. The maximization of production is achieved through promoting technological change or through wars of conquest. Not all societies give these goals equal priority. A society's preference depends on its degree of stratification. Highly stratified societies with powerful elites, Lenski posits, tend to emphasize political stability, those less stratified favor maximizing production (Lenski, 1966, p. 42).

5.   Inequality is present in every human society.

Economic goods and services are not distributed equally to all members of society—some always get more than others. Lenski believes that the distribution of goods and services (as well as prestige) is largely determined by power. Taking his cue from Weber, Lenski defines power as the ability of a person or group to achieve their goals even when opposed by others (Lenski, 1966, p. 45). Also consistent with Weber, Lenski asserts that stratification is a "multi-dimensional phenomenon," that is, populations are ranked along various dimensions such as occupation, education, property, racial-ethnic status, age, and gender (Lenski, 1966, pp. 74–80). Lenski refers to each of these dimensions as a "class system." Class systems are "a hierarchy of classes ranked in terms of a single criterion" (Lenski, 1966, p. 79). Thus, "African-American" is a particular class within the American racial-ethnic class system, "working class" is a particular class within the American occupational class system.

An individual's position in each of the relevant hierarchies (and these vary by society) determines their class, and their class will often affect their access to goods and services as well as the prestige accorded to them by others. The members of each class share material interests with one another and these interests are often the basis for class consciousness (or awareness of common position and interests)[4] and "hostility toward other classes" (Lenski, 1966, p. 76).[5]

"One of the great advantages of a conscious recognition of class systems as a distinct level of organization is that we are led to see that the struggle for power and privilege involves not only struggles between individuals and classes, it also involves struggles between class systems, and thus between different principles of distribution" (Lenski, 1966, p. 81). Lenski points out that the Civil Rights movement in the United States can be properly viewed as a struggle to reduce the importance of the racial-ethnic class system as a basis of distribution. Class systems differ in terms of their complexity, the degree of mobility possible within the system, the importance of the system in terms of the distribution of goods and services, as well as the degree of hostility between the classes within the system (Lenski, 1966, p. 82). "Viewed in their totality, distributive systems resemble a system of wheels within wheels. The complexity of these systems varies considerably and seems to be largely a function of the societies' level of technology" (Lenski, 1966, p. 84).

6. Goods and services within societies are distributed on the basis of need (subsistence goods) and power (surplus goods).

There are two basic "laws" of distribution, and while they are, on the surface at least, somewhat contradictory, both are consistent with Lenski's postulates on the nature of man and society. As you recall, according to Lenski human beings are social animals and need to live in cooperation with others to most efficiently achieve their needs. This leads him to posit that "enlightened self-interest" will lead humans to "share the product of their labors to the extent required to ensure the survival and continued productivity of those others whose actions are necessary or beneficial to themselves" (Lenski, 1966, p. 44). However, Lenski also states that human beings are primarily motivated by self-interest. This leads him to posit that any goods over and above the minimum needed to keep the majority of producers alive and productive will be distributed on the basis of power. This has enormous consequences for the degree of inequality within societies.

7. Elites rule through a variety of means, but force undergirds all power and authority.

Force is a very inefficient and expensive way to maintain order. "Though force is the most effective instrument for seizing power in a society, and though it always remains the foundation of any system of inequality, it is not the most effective instrument for retaining and exploiting a position of power and deriving the maximum benefit from it" (Lenski, 1966, p. 51). Thus, those who seize power will soon move to "legitimize" their rule and transform force into authority (Lenski, 1966, p. 52). Power is legitimated through three major institutions. First, of course, is through the rule of law. Lenski notes that laws are often written so as to benefit positions of power, and since they appear to embody "abstract principles of justice," are quite effective in gaining widespread acceptance and compliance from the vast majority of men.

A second method of legitimation employed by elites is through shaping public opinion through institutions such as educational institutions, religious institutions, and the media. Many of those who work in these institutions are beholden to elite owners or donors; if not directly dependent on elites, many working in these institutions are open to their threats or blandishments. Consensus and coercion, Lenski points out, are far more closely related than many appreciate. Like Mills before him, he points out that "coercive power can often be used to create a new consensus" (Lenski, 1966, p. 53).

The process of legitimation is facilitated, Lenski notes, by the press of daily events on the lives of the vast majority of people. Most are engaged full-time in making a living; they have neither the time nor the financial resources to become involved in the political arena for long. While it is possible to arouse the majority in time of crisis or political revolution, the necessity of work, family, and private life continually reasserts itself. Consequently, the elite or their officers usually handle the affairs of state (Lenski, 1966, p. 54).

As force shifts to authority and manipulation there are some important changes that occur in the distribution of goods and services that ultimately have far-reaching effect on the degree of inequality within societies. Elites are caught in the rules of their own game so to speak. With the rule of law at least some of their actions must be consistent with prevailing conceptions of justice and morality. To act otherwise would be to jeopardize their legitimation. Secondly, following Vilfredo Pareto, there is a shift in the personality and character of the elite from those comfortable with the use of force and power to those more comfortable with "cunning," manipulation, and diplomacy.

In addition, Lenski asserts that a shift of power from force to manipulation and authority also involves the institutionalization of authority. By this Lenski means the rise of bureaucracy, where authority becomes a socially acceptable form of power that inheres in the office rather than the individual. Officers who enjoy such authority rule on the basis of their office rather than their personal characteristics. Rule becomes impersonal and not easily challenged. In addition, Lenski writes, such institutionalized power is likely to be far more decentralized than the centralized rule of founding elites (Lenski, 1966, p. 56). Competing power centers are allowed to exist and develop as long as they remain subject to the rule of law.

It is also in this period of transition from force to authority that retainers and the middle class arise. This middle stratum consists of public officials, priests, soldiers, craftsmen, merchants and others who serve as overseers and technicians in the service of elites. The chief function of this middle stratum is to separate the surplus from the producers (Lenski, 1966, pp. 62–63). Over time, Lenski posits, the relations between the political elite and this middle stratum change, as these classes begin to acquire some of the power and privileges of the elite. "This is not difficult since it is their normal function to act on behalf of the elite. Powers delegated often become powers lost; once lost they are not easily recovered" (Lenski, 1966, p. 63).

According to Lenski, the cumulative effect of these changes on the governance of sociocultural systems is marked. The movement from force to authority, the rise of manipulation and cunning as techniques of power, as well as the rise of a middle stratum that begins to appropriate some power and privileges to itself, all strengthen a move toward constitutional government. As defined by Lenski constitutional government is a system in which the political elite makes some concessions in the distribution of resources in return for legitimation and consent of the governed.

8. Societies are remarkably stable systems that tend to resist change.

Societies can be remarkably stable over time. Hunting and gathering societies existed with little technological, population, or structural change for thousands (if not millions) of years. Ancient civilizations that depended upon river irrigation for their agriculture were also remarkably stable. These stable societies can be characterized as successful attempts at striking a balance between the consumption of energy and their finite biological and physical environments. In other words, one of the major reasons for the stability of many social and cultural elements in many societies appears to be their adaptive value to the sociocultural system (Lenski et al., 1991, p. 48).

But there are other causes for the remarkable stability found in many sociocultural systems. As is often remarked, human beings are creatures of habit, and this means that we are very reluctant to change. In addition, tradition or custom—the "eternal yesteryear" of Weber— has a very powerful hold on individuals within a society. Tradition and habit cause men and women to accept existing institutional arrangements and distribution systems as "right and natural," no matter the fairness to themselves or others (Lenski, 1966, p. 32). Through the socialization process we have all been taught the values, norms, morality, attitudes, beliefs, and ideologies of the culture. It is through this process that such norms and values take on an almost "sacred" character, thus becoming extremely resistant to change (Lenski et al., 1991, p. 50).

Another important impediment to sociocultural change is the need for some standardization (Lenski et al., 1991, p. 48). This is due to the fact that most sociocultural change is built upon or added to existing structures and institutions. While newer innovations may offer many advantages, past adaptations of the society may prohibit the widespread adaptation of these innovations. Lenski mentions driving on the right side of the road as an example.[6]

Another reason for sociocultural stability over time is the systemic character of the society itself (Lenski et al., 1991, p. 50). Most of the elements of a sociocultural system are linked to others. Change in one element often causes change in many others (in a system, as the ecologists are fond of telling us, you can't change *one* thing). An example of innovation causing extensive system change is the recent movement of married women to the outside labor force, which then causes extensive adjustment in all major institutions (family, government, distribution systems) as well as in many of our cultural values and ideologies. As a result of the systemic character of society, members as well as organized groups within a society often resist such innovations (as the recent struggles over women's liberation attest).

Other causes of sociocultural continuity mentioned by Lenski are related to the ones already given: adaptation, tradition and habit, standardization, and the systemic character of society. For example, Lenski mentions costs (both monetary and psychic) as a major impediment to the adaptation of innovation. In this connection, he offers as an example the costs in terms of dollars, time, and energy it would take for Americans to change to the metric system (Lenski et al., 1991, p. 49). But the resistance to metric on the part of Americans is clearly related to tradition, personal habit, systemic character, and standardization as well. Rather than as an impediment to change, cost is better conceived of as a primary factor in the individual decision making process of adaptation. When confronted with innovation the individual performs a cost/benefit analysis to reveal if the costs of adapting the innovation are worth the anticipated benefits (Harris, 1979, p. 61). Lenski places the individual members of the society as the prime actors in adaptation (Lenski et al., 1991, p. 58), cost-benefit is the calculus they use in making their decisions (Lenski, 2005, p. 64).

9.   **Societies evolve in response to changes in their natural or social environments.**

Sociocultural change is of two types, innovation and extinction. The first involves adding new elements such as technologies, social practices, institutions, or beliefs to the system. The second type of change, of course, is the elimination of old elements in the system. While extinction certainly occurs, the process of sociocultural evolution is predominantly a cumulative process, that is, change and innovation are added far more to the system than are older elements eliminated. This, Lenski adds, is one reason why sociocultural systems have grown more complex over time (Lenski et al., 1991, p. 48).

It is also important to again note that sociocultural innovation is based on the alteration of existing structures and behavior patterns. In fact, Lenski states, there are ultimately only three major factors determining the characteristics of sociocultural systems: (1) human's genetic heritage; (2) the biological, physical, and social environment; and (3) "the influence of prior social and cultural characteristics of society itself" (Lenski et al., 1991, pp. 17–18). The force of historical experience therefore plays a major role in shaping social institutions and thought.

The rate of innovation and change greatly varies across different societies. Lenski identifies several factors that influence this rate. The first is "the amount of information a society already possesses" (Lenski et al., 1991, pp. 54–55). A society with a larger store of cultural information is often able to combine new innovation with older cultural elements, thus amplifying and propagating the innovation throughout the sociocultural system. One need only think of the recent innovation of the Internet, and the myriad of uses made of it by governments, educational institutions, research labs, corporations, and a host of other entities and individuals. Thus, the rate of change is accelerated in advanced industrial societies, and as the store of technical information increases it speeds up the potential for change even further (Lenski, 2005, p. 66).

A second factor that serves to vary the rate of innovation is population size (Lenski et al., 1991, p. 55). Here Lenski is referring to the simple fact that the more people within a population, the more potential innovators and the greater the number of people searching for solutions to a particular problem. However, he is also referring to the fact that large populations tend to be highly organized, have access to more varied kinds of information, and also are faced by more complex problems that demand technological or social change.

A third factor that affects the rate of change and innovation within a society is the stability of the physical and biological environment itself. "The greater the rate of environmental change, the greater the pressure for change in culture and social organization" (Lenski et al., 1991, p. 55). Changes in the physical and biological environment can be due to natural processes (say, climate change during the interglacial period some 11,000 years ago), or occasioned by the actions of sociocultural systems themselves (say, desertification, which has occurred throughout human history, or the global warming of today).

One of the most important factors that affects the rate of change within a society "is the extent of that society's contact with other societies" (Lenski et al., 1991, p. 55). Isolated societies, or those with very little contact with others, experience very slow rates of innovation (Lenski et al., 1991, p. 68). While environmental necessity is the key to understanding "pristine" change—change that occurs in isolation from contact with other societies—the rapid adoption of most technologies and social practices are done through borrowing technologies and practices from other societies, or cultural diffusion (Lenski et al., 1991, p. 51).

A fifth factor in determining the rate of innovation is the character of the physical and biological environment. Some environments, such as the arctic or desert regions, simply cannot support innovations like agriculture. But the environment has more subtle effects as well (fans of Jared Diamond's *Guns, Germs and Steel*[7] take note):

> The absence of vital resources, such as adequate water supply or accessible metallic ores, can also hinder innovation, as can endemic diseases and parasites that deplete people's energy. Topography has played an important role in shaping patterns of intersocietal communications. Oceans, deserts, and mountain ranges have all prevented or seriously impeded the flow of information between societies, while navigable rivers and open plains have facilitated it. Considering the importance of diffusion, enormous differences in the rate of innovation can be explained by this factor alone. (Lenski et al., 1991, p. 56)

Lenski also notes that there are "fundamental" innovations that have an affect on the overall rate of innovation within a society as well (Lenski et al., 1991, pp. 56–57). By fundamental, Lenski is referring to innovations like plant cultivation, writing, the plow, or the invention of the steam engine. Adapting such fundamental innovations causes rapid and often revolutionary changes in many other areas of the sociocultural system.

The seventh factor affecting the rate of innovation noted by Lenski is the society's attitudes and ideologies toward change and innovation. These ideologies and attitudes vary by a society's prior experience with change, as well as the dominant ideology of the society (or the ideology of the elite). A society dominated by capitalist ideology, Lenski notes, is far more supportive of innovation and change than societies dominated by Confucianism or Islamic fundamentalism (Lenski et al., 1991, pp. 57–62).

Finally, Lenski notes, technological innovation itself has a tendency to occur at an accelerating rate (Lenski et al., 1991, p. 57). This is because technological information, like other forms of cultural information, can often be recombined to produce novel invention. In addition, technological innovation is related to several other factors affecting the rate of innovation discussed above—population growth, environmental and biological change, increasing cultural contact—as well as affecting the attitudes and ideologies of societies regarding change itself.

Sociocultural change occurs as a consequence of individual members of society making adaptive changes to their natural and social environments. Of course, not all people have equal power in the decision making process; "who decides" often depends on the nature of the choice and one's position in the stratification system. As a consequence many important decisions are made by a few, and these few may well choose alternatives that enhance or bolster their interests rather than the interests of the total society. It is, after all, an imperfect social system (Lenski et al., 1991, pp. 58–59). Structural elites acting in their own interests therefore provide positive and negative reinforcement for the adoption or extinction of technological and social change. This feedback can often be decisive in determining whether change is propagated throughout the sociocultural system or whether it is extinguished.

10. Changes in subsistence technology and population have far ranging consequences for human organization, cultural beliefs, and values.

Two types of change are of tremendous importance: changes in basic subsistence technologies, and changes in population levels (Lenski et al., 1991, p. 54). This configuration is, of course, identical to Harris's infrastructure. Lenski, however, has a "broad" interpretation of the principle of infrastructural determinism while Harris's tends to be somewhat "strict." R. Brian Ferguson (1995) had this to say about the difference between the two interpretations. "The strict interpretation holds that all sociocultural phenomena are to be explained with reference to the infrastructure; and the broad interpretation is that the infrastructure is the primary, general determinant of sociocultural form, but that other causal relationships must be sought to explain many sociocultural patterns" (p. 22). Ferguson goes on to argue that (a) the broad interpretation makes for a theory capable of integrating a wide range of research and findings [which Lenski's certainly does]; and (b)

Harris himself tends to be strict in his theoretical formulations and somewhat broader in practical analysis.

Technology and population, of course, are closely intertwined. Increase the production of food and more children can be allowed to live (Lenski, 1966, p. 64). Especially in preindustrial societies where children are economic assets, increases in subsistence production inevitably lead to increases in population (Lenski et al., 1991, pp. 172–173). Better methods and technologies of contraception allow individuals to apply preventive checks on their fertility (Lenski et al., 1991, p. 54). Population level and growth, on the other hand, put pressure on the biological and physical environments as well as providing more direct stimulus for further technological development. Not only are the two closely linked, however, but both exert strong impact on the rest of the sociocultural system.

In accordance with Goldschmidt, Lenski posits the existence of several different modes of production throughout human history, beginning with hunter and gatherer, and then on to horticulture, agrarian, and industrial.[8] Table 4.1 displays this classification scheme of different modes of production (that can be further broken down into "simple" and "advanced"), which is based on the technology and social practices used to draw subsistence and other primary resources from the environment—that is, such factors as metallurgy, use of the plow, iron, and the use of fossil fuel.

Technology and population combined set strong limits on widespread social organizational characteristics as well as on ideas and ideologies. These limits include maximum community size and complexity, the division of labor, the degree of inequality, the degree of military power that the society can project, complexity of stratification systems,

Table 4.1: Criteria for Classifying Primary Types of Human Societies

Type:	Cultivate	Metal	Plow	Iron	Fossil Fuel	Hi-Tech
Hunt & Gather	–	–	–	–	–	–
S. Horticulture	+	–	–	–	–	–
A. Horticulture	+	+	–	–	–	–
S. Agrarian	+	+	+	–	–	–
A. Agrarian	+	+	+	+	–	–
Industrial	+	+	+	+	+	–
Hyperindustrial	+	+	+	+	+	+

From Lenski, Lenski, & Nolan. Human Societies: An Introduction to Macrosociology, 1991, 6th edition, p. 71. The + symbol indicates that the practice is widespread in the type of society, the – sign that it is not. The categories "Hi-Tech" and "Hyperindustrial" have been added to this chart by this author.

and the overall wealth of the society (Lenski, 1966, pp.47–48; Lenski et al., 1991, p. 60). Advances in subsistence technology are important because they are often related to improvements in other technologies such as transportation and communications, all of which leads to greater societal growth and complexity. The demographics of population, over and above sheer size, can also have dramatic impact on the rest of the sociocultural system. Such demographic properties as age and sex composition, birth and death rates, density, and patterns of migration, all have potential for far reaching impact on social structure and cultural beliefs and values (Lenski et al., 1991, p. 29).[9]

Lenski considers population and subsistence production critical in understanding sociocultural systems because these two variables are the principle means by which society regulates the flow of energy from its environment. Increases in the food supply made possible by innovations in subsistence technology is a necessary precondition for high population levels, both of which are preconditions for significant increases in the complexity of a society (Lenski et al., 1991, p. 60). The resulting complexity, of course, creates many new problems for sociocultural systems, all of which call for further technological, social, and cultural change (Lenski et al., 1991, pp. 61–62).

11. The more intensive the subsistence technology, the greater the surplus, the greater the surplus, the greater the inequality.

As reported before (#6), Lenski asserts that goods and services are distributed within a society on the basis of need and power. The enlightened self-interests of humans lead them to equitably distribute goods and services to productive classes in order to ensure their survival and continued productivity. However, Lenski posits, any surplus is likely to be divided in accordance with self-interests, that is, on the basis of social power. The major focus of *Power and Privilege* was in developing an ecological theory of stratification. His first hypothesis in this theory predicts "that in the simplest societies, or those which are technologically the most primitive, the goods and services available will be distributed on the basis of need" (Lenski, 1966, p. 46).

As technology and productivity increases, Lenski goes on, a portion of the new goods and services will go toward necessary population growth and feeding a larger population. However, with technological development and subsequent increases in productivity, a larger surplus of goods and services will also be produced. Lenski's second hypothesis predicts "that with technological advance, an increasing proportion of goods and services available to a society will be distributed on the basis of power (Lenski, 1966, p. 46). If true, then when examining sociocultural systems we should see that the greater the technological advance (as measured by productivity), the greater the inequality in the distribution of goods and services within the society.

Lenski offers several caveats before going on to test his basic theory. Several factors may well lead to "secondary variation" in the degree of inequality within a society. Technological development is not the only factor that is related to productivity and the creation of surplus goods and services within a society. Since the nature of the physical environment also has some effect on productivity, he predicts that environments would have some effect on inequality as well. Specifically, an environment with a greater endowment of natural resources will enable the society to achieve greater surpluses, thus increasing the amount of inequality within the society (Lenski, 1966, p. 48). Another factor that may also affect the degree of inequality, according to Lenski, is "the military participation ratio." Following Stanislaw Andrzejewski, Lenski asserts that the higher the proportion of males serving in the military, the less the inequality (Lenski, 1966, p. 49). A final source of secondary variation in the degree of inequality within a given societal type is the political cycle. In societies in which elites have sought legitimation through constitutional government (Point #7 above), some lessening of inequality can be predicted (Lenski, 1966, pp. 49–50). Lenski summarizes his theory of inequality:

> Though this theory predicts that variations in technology are the most important single determinant of variations in distribution, it does not hypothesize that they are the only determinant. Three others are specifically singled out: (1) environmental differences, (2) variations in the military participation ratio, (3) variations in the degree of constitutionalism. In addition, since this is not a closed theory, it is assumed that other factors also exercise an influence. (Lenski, 1966, p. 90)

Lenski proceeds to test this theory of inequality through examining ethnographies and histories of societies based on different subsistence techniques of ascending order of technological efficiency: Hunting and gathering, simple horticultural, advanced horticultural, agrarian, and industrial societies.[10] In *Power and Privilege*, Lenski finds increasing degrees of inequality up to and including early industrial society. At this stage in development, he finds the degree of inequality peaking out and then beginning to lessen as industrial societies mature.

There is an incredible concentration of wealth and power in agrarian societies because in such societies the state is seen as the private property of the rulers and a small governing class. This allows them to use the powers of the state to expropriate the economic surplus from the majority of the population. Lenski (1966) reports that up to 50 percent of all the income in agrarian societies was collected by the top 1 or 2 percent of the population (p. 309). This represents far greater inequality than his estimated "15.5 percent" of income that the top 2 percent of the population in American society receives on an annual basis (p. 310). He adds that *income* inequality appears to be even less in the Soviet Union.

In succeeding editions of *Human Societies* Lenski continues to monitor inequalities in industrial societies. In 1993 he estimates that the top 10 percent of income earners in Western democracies appear to receive from 20 to 30 percent of all of the income (p. 336). In sum, in mature industrial societies the lower social classes appear to materially benefit more than in agrarian societies both in absolute and relative terms. Elites appear to receive far less of a proportion of the nation's income. Lenski concludes that mature industrial societies thus represent a reversal of a long-standing evolutionary trend in which inequality increased with technological development (Lenski, 1966, p. 308).

Lenski (1966, pp. 313–325) attributes this lessening of inequality to a variety of factors not directly anticipated in his original hypothesis.[11] The first and perhaps most important necessity is a large administrative and technical structure in order to coordinate the sophisticated technology, great numbers of people, and elements of the increasingly complex culture (Lenski, 1966, p. 313–314). Because of their knowledge and expertise, higher administrative and technical positions must be given a degree of latitude in the performance of their duties. ("Powers delegated often become powers lost.") They also demand a larger share of the surplus.

A second factor Lenski points to is related to the rapidly growing surplus itself. By allocating a greater share to the lower classes the elite may be able to buy worker allegiance and commitment, thus promoting further economic growth (Lenski, 1966, pp. 314–315). This may be especially true in an economy that relies heavily upon the productivity of workers whose qualitative output is not so easily measurable. If allocating a greater relative share to the lower and middle classes will still increase the absolute share of the elite, it may well be worth the sacrifice. An elite in such an expanding economy, Lenski also points out, may well become satiated with material rewards alone—the first million dollars will mean far more to consumption and life styles than the second million dollars. Such elites may well be willing to sacrifice some portion of further rewards in return for a reduction in class hostilities, greater economic or political security, or even more leisure time (Lenski, 1966, p. 315).

A third factor behind the lessening of inequality can be attributed to changes in population and production dynamics in mature industrial societies. In the past, with the exception of the surplus that was drained off by the elite (to create what we call civilization), increases in productivity were accompanied by increases in human population. This is because children in traditional societies were productive assets, a way of intensifying production itself. Breaking the link between children and production, such reforms as child labor laws and the provision of economic security in old age changes the dynamic between the two. With the introduction of modern birth control, people can now more easily and safely control their numbers; increases in productivity can be converted to increases in per capita income. As an additional bonus, a declining birth rate among the lower classes reduces competitive pressures among workers, allowing even the semi-skilled to demand more equitable wages (Lenski, 1966, pp. 315–316).

A fourth factor that Lenski identifies as contributing to growing income equality is the expansion of human knowledge and the concomitant increase in the division of labor. Skilled labor is in a much better bargaining position than the unskilled labor that dominated earlier societies. "Because of the great functional utility of so much of the new knowledge, a host of occupational specialists have appeared who are not interchangeable to any great degree" (Lenski, 1966, p. 318). Such labor can demand a greater share of the surplus.

The final factor in the lessening inequality of mature industrial societies that Lenski examines is a rise in ideologies that advocate more economic equality. Such ideologies would include the rise of Socialist parties in Europe as well as the liberal ideology behind the establishment of the Welfare State in the United States. These ideologies are associated with the rise of constitutional government and democracies in which political power is much more dispersed. As a result, governments have become more representative of the broader population and much more active in addressing internal inequalities.

There are several cautions regarding Lenski's findings: First, industrial societies were most "equal" (or less unequal) in income. As Lenski notes, inequalities in wealth are far more significant in all societies. Second, a good part of the income equality of industrial societies that Lenski reported occurred in the former Soviet Union. Some of that country's income data were seriously misleading in the 1960s; rubles earned by party leaders were far more valuable than those earned by the average citizen; exclusive access to stores selling foreign goods was assured by membership in the party.[12] Perhaps more importantly, the Soviet Union is no more, and along with its collapse there has been a weakening of ideologies favoring income redistribution throughout the world. Third, Lenski's study of the United States economy was done in the 1960s, at the tail end of what economists now call the "Great Compression." It was a period of time when, in response to the speculative excesses of the 1920s and the Great Depression of the 1930s, U.S. incomes were perhaps at their most egalitarian point in history. Finally, while Lenski found decreasing income inequality within the U.S. he did find increasing inequality in the world as a whole. Lenski points out that *"[t]he gap between rich and poor societies has been widening ever since the start of the industrial era"* [emphasis in the original text] (Lenski et al., 1991, p. 337). With increasing globalization (and I would add, the growth of capital), he contends, this trend is bound to intensify.

12. There is a process of selection in the world system that favors larger, more powerful societies at the expense of smaller, less powerful ones.

As previously stated, sociocultural change is largely a cumulative process, which is the major factor in the growth of the complexity and size of societies over the course of human history (Lenski et al., 1991, p. 48). But to fully appreciate the process of sociocultural evolution, you must recognize that it includes both continuity and change (Lenski et al., 1991, pp. 65–66). The vast majority of societies have experienced very little change over the course of their history (Lenski et al., 1991, p. 46). But in the global system as a whole, societies have gotten larger, developed more sophisticated methods of exploiting their environments, and developed more complex divisions of labor (Lenski, 2005, p. 31). This paradox has created some confusion among both supporters and critics of social evolutionary theory. How, Lenski rhetorically asks, can the global system of societies change so radically, particularly in the last 10,000 years, when individual societies appear so resistant to change? The answer is that social evolution exists on two different levels, and that these two levels—individual societies and the global system of societies—follow divergent evolutionary paths (Lenski, 2005, p. 32).

At the global system level, there has been a dramatic reduction in the number of societies in the last 10,000 years, due to a process that Lenski identifies as "inter-societal selection." Societies that have grown in size and technology have also grown in complexity and military power; and this has allowed them to prevail in conflict over territory and other resources with societies that have maintained more traditional sociocultural patterns (Lenski et al., 1991, p. 47). Successful adaptations are spread through social contact, and military and economic conquest. Societies that adopted innovations that led to increases in productive capacity, population growth, structural complexity, and military power are those that have survived to transmit their culture and institutional patterns (Lenski et al., 1991, p. 63). At the individual level, societies respond to changes in their natural and social environments, which, in combination with their distinct histories, produces the innovative adaptations, some of which get passed on to other societies within the global system and become part of the intersocietal selection process. Sociocultural evolution therefore operates on two distinct levels, within individual societies and within the world system of societies. The two processes combined determine "which societies and which cultures survive and which become extinct, and the role that each of the survivors plays within the world system" (Lenski et al., 1991, p. 66).

EXCURSUS: INEQUALITY REVISITED

Much has happened in the years since Lenski tested his inequality hypothesis, particularly in regard to intrasocietal inequality. Table 4.2 displays the growing income disparity between each fifth of the American population between 1977 and 1999. As can be seen the share of all

Table 4.2: Growing Income Disparity

Household Groups	Share of All Income		Average After-tax Income Estimated		Change
	1977	1999	1977	1999	
One-fifth with lowest income	5.7%	5.2%	$10,000.00	$8,800.00	–12.0%
Next lowest one-fifth	11.5%	9.7%	$22,100.00	$20,000.00	–9.5%
Middle one-fifth	16.4%	14.7%	$32,400.00	$31,400.00	–3.1%
Next highest one-fifth	22.8%	21.3%	$42,600.00	$45,100.00	5.9%
One-fifth with highest income	44.2%	50.4%	$74,000.00	$102,300.00	38.3%
1 Percent with highest income	7.3%	12.9%	$234,700.00	$515,600.00	119.7%

Source: *Congressional Budget Office Data Analyzed by Center and Policy Priorities.* Reprinted in the *New York Times*, September 5, 1999, appearing in Kevin Phillips, *Wealth and Democracy*, 2002, p. 129.

income for the bottom four fifths has declined over these years, the bottom three fifths actually experiencing a decline in absolute terms as measured in constant dollars of after-tax income. At the same time, the top one-fifth with the highest income had their percentage going from 44.2 percent of all wages to 50.4 percent. The highest 1 percent had their income share go from 7.3 percent to 12.9 percent, more than doubling their after tax income.

So unequal has it become that the *New York Times* began the 1999 article on the growing gulf by drawing a contrast that could well be from the Gilded Age itself. "The gap between rich and poor has grown into an economic chasm so wide that this year the richest 2.7 million Americans, the top 1 percent, will have as many after-tax dollars to spend as the bottom 100 million" (quoted in Phillips, 2002, p. 103).

Wealth, of course, has always been unevenly distributed, and again the concentration of wealth has been growing since Lenski originally tested his technology-surplus-inequality hypothesis. Table 4.3 displays the Top 1 Percent's Share of Household Wealth from 1922 to 1997. As can be seen, after a sharp drop after 1929, when their share of the wealth plummeted from 44.3 percent to 33.3 percent, there has been a rapid increase since 1981, climbing from 24.8 percent of all household wealth to 40.1 percent.

Table 4.3: Top 1% Share of Household Wealth, 1922–1997

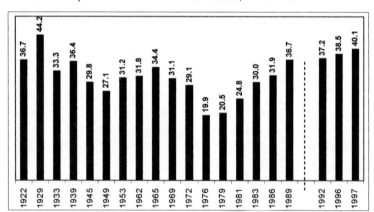

Source: Edward Wolff, *Top Heavy*, 1996, New Series Household data, pp. 78–79 (for years 1922–89 and "Recent Trends in Wealth Ownership," 1998 (for years 1992–97) appearing in Kevin Phillips, *Wealth and Democracy*, 2002, p. 123.

In reviewing the concentration of wealth in American society from its (Western) beginnings to 2002, Kevin Phillips (no wild-eyed radical but a staid Nixon Republican) agrees with Lenski that the American zenith in inequality was in the Gilded Age of early capitalism. However, he notes that since the 1970s American inequality—now higher than any industrial nation in the world on several measures (p. 111)—has been growing rapidly and will soon be approaching the levels of the late Gilded Age (Phillips, 2002, p. 122). He remarks (unconsciously echoing Lenski's hypothesis): "Over two centuries, the greater the complexity attained by the U.S. economy—in size, technology, and financial sophistication—the loftier the distance between its uppermost and bottom layers" (p. 110).

It would seem that Lenski's technology-surplus-inequality hypothesis is still very viable. At the very least, higher technology leading to a greater surplus is an enabling factor behind growing inequality. It is interesting to note that the top 20 percent in hyperindustrial societies are now collecting national income in the proportions that were previously attained by the elite of agrarian societies, though agrarian elites were only 1 to 2 percent of the population.[13]

Several of Lenski's mitigating factors to greater inequality are of direct relevance to this top 20 percent attaining a greater share of the national income. These factors would include (a) the need for administrative and technical specialists to run a complex society; (b) the division of labor in which at least some with special skills and education can bargain for more of a share; and (c) the investment by the elite of part of their relative share in order to increase their absolute share of the surplus. These factors alone would be enough to explain the increase in the number of well off in the *top* tier. However, Lenski's other mitigating factors, those that he posited would lead to increases in the amount and relative share of surplus distributed to those at the *bottom* of the income pyramid, may well have been of a short-term historical nature.

While Gross Domestic Product has been growing significantly since the late 1970s, general social health as measured by such factors as education, infant mortality, and child poverty has actually declined (Phillips, 2002, p. 167). This is because all of the factors that Lenski cited in 1966 that led to a significant amount of the surplus being redistributed to the bottom of the income pyramid have been annulled. As Harris stated (and Malthus anticipated), industrialization initially produced a de-coupling of population and production; that is, many in the lower and middle classes found it in their interest to limit their fertility with their increased wages. This demographic transition may have pro-

duced some temporary gain in income for the lower classes by lessening competition for jobs. However, this temporary gain was quickly
wiped out with increased rates of immigration, factory and office automation, and now both the outsourcing of many American jobs as well
as the increased competition from developing nations. For a time the
increasing division of labor did lead to greater bargaining power on the
part of the working classes; however, the increasing detailed division of
labor has led to a de-skilling and a decline in their bargaining position.
At the same time low level (and low pay) service jobs are on the rise,
and union membership and power have undergone a sharp decline. Finally, while Lenski points to the increasing role of government in addressing inequality, since his writing there has been a spread of ideologies that seek to limit government action on behalf of those at the bottom of the wealth pyramid.[14] Since the mid-sixties inequality has grown
in the United States as progressive income tax rates have been gutted,
corporate and capital gains taxes have been slashed, and corporate profits, capital gains, and executive salaries have soared.[15]

U.S. corporate profits have, of course, risen dramatically in the
last 20 years. The wealthiest 10 percent of the population owned 91
percent of all corporate and business assets in 1992 (Phillips, 2002, p.
150). In 1950 corporate taxes accounted for 26.5 percent of total federal
receipts. By 2000 they accounted for only 10.2 percent. In that same
time period, payroll taxes climbed from 6.9 percent of total receipts to
31.1 percent (Phillips, 2002, p. 149). Capital gains income climbed
dramatically in the same time period, rising in constant dollars from
$74.6 billion in 1980 to $507 billion in 1999 (Phillips, 2002, p. 130).
The wealthy receive the vast majority of capital gains, and they are, of
course, taxed at a much lower rate than income from working (Phillips,
2002, p. 150). The effective federal tax rate for a median family rose
from 5.30 percent in 1948 to 24.63 percent in 1990. The top 1 percent
of families effective tax rate declined from 76.9 percent in 1948 to 26.7
percent in 1989 (Phillips, 2002, p. 96).

As in agrarian societies, wealth and income are very much concentrated at the top in hyperindustrial society. While there has been a significant redistribution of wealth among the top 20 percent or so, very
little of the surplus appears to be distributed to those at the bottom. The
fact that that top has broadened to 10 or 20 percent of the population
rather than the 1 or 2 percent in agrarian societies gives the retainer
class (those professionals and administrators who are midlevel within
the bureaucratic hierarchy) an economic stake and thus loyalty to the
system. However the existence of this retainer class cannot be a cause
of great celebration among the vast majority.

ABOUT LENSKI[16]

Gerhard Lenski was born in Washington, D.C., on August 13, 1924, to Gerhard Sr. and Christine (Umhau) Lenski. His father, Gerhard Sr., earned a Ph.D. in history and was a Lutheran minister. His Washington congregation consisted of a mix of people—from congressmen, people working at foreign embassies (including a few ambassadors), government bureaucrats and clerks, as well as blue-collar workers. Many of these people, as well as his father's academic friends, would end up at the family dinner table. Lenski recalls Washington as "a wonderful place to grow up in the 1930s. New Deal politics were exciting, and my parents and relatives loved discussing and debating the issues of the day."

Lenski recalls that the Washington public schools he attended in the 1930s were excellent. His friends from both school and his father's congregation cut across class lines. His interest in stratification, however, really came alive through his experiences at Yale and in the military. Lenski began Yale in 1941 on scholarship and work-study, working 20 hours a week in the kitchen his freshman year and in the geology workshop during his sophomore year. In these first two years at Yale he had good opportunity to observe "the life of the upper class." In 1943 Lenski left school to serve with the U.S. Army Air Force as an enlisted man, eventually earning the rank of sergeant. In the army his fellow soldiers and friends were all from working class or rural families. "It would be hard to exaggerate the contrast between these two worlds, and only a dolt could not be fascinated by the contrast."

His interest in comparative sociology was also rooted in his formative years. An occasional dinner guest in his parent's home was a man who had fought in the Russo-Japanese war and who told the young man of the horrors of the experience. Another frequent guest, his father's dissertation advisor, Ernst Correl—a former student of Max Weber's—also stimulated this interest. In addition, there were the friends from other places, many with radically different ways of looking at the world. One of his friends in high school "was the son of a staff member in the German embassy with whom I had many lively discussions about Nazism, while in my freshman year at Yale, my best friend was the son of a German refugee who offered a rather different perspective on Nazism."

The military also gave him an appreciation of different cultures. During his three years with the Eighth Air Force he spent most of his time in England, but also was stationed briefly in France and the Azores. "While in England, I came to know a number of English peo-

ple very well and even spent a month billeted with an English family
while on assignment with the Royal Air Force, so I had many opportunities to see close up how different our two seemingly similar societies
actually were."

As a young man Lenski began a lifelong fascination with the Soviet Union. In particular, he was interested in the contrast of the pro-
fessed ideals of Soviet communism and the "grim totalitarian reality"
of Stalinism—the purges and show trials, and the concentration camps
of the Gulag. Lenski was also struck by the brutal treatment of Russian
war prisoners upon their return to the Soviet Union after the war. Later,
as a sociologist, Lenski made many contacts among Eastern European
sociologists, and traveled there during the Cold War on several occa-
sions.

There are two other strands of Lenski's sociology to be accounted
for in this brief sketch. The first is his obvious bent toward historical
sociology. Lenski asserts that he came by this interest as a child in his
reading of Genesis. He remembers being frustrated that the Bible had
so little to say about what life was like in early times. In high school he
discovered H.G. Wells's *The Outline of History*. Eventually history was
to become one of the foundations of his sociology. The second influence on his sociology, evolution, was initiated in his freshman college
course in geology. It was here where Lenski got his "first serious introduction" to evolutionary theory. However, in graduate school he was
discouraged from pursuing study in social evolution, as such theory
was widely discredited in sociology, and functionalism was hailed as
the "coming thing."

After completing his service in the Army in 1945, Lenski returned
to Yale on the GI Bill, where he earned his B.A. in sociology in 1947
and his Ph.D. in sociology in 1950. Lenski was much influenced in his
graduate studies by A. B. Hollingshead, author of *Elmtown's Youth*.
Hollingshead became his dissertation director, providing Lenski "in-
valuable" advice in Lenski's first major research project focusing on a
Connecticut mill town.

Starting out as a postdoctoral instructor at the University of
Michigan, Lenski became an assistant professor in 1954, and an associate professor in 1959. In 1961 he published *The Religious Factor*, a
study of the influence of religion on behavior and attitudes. In 1963 he
became a full professor at Michigan before he moved to the University
of North Carolina at Chapel Hill. In 1966 he published *Power and
Privilege*, a study in social stratification, and in 1970, the first edition
of *Human Societies*. Beginning with the second edition, Lenski co-
authored the work with his wife Jean Lenski. In the 6th edition in 1991,

they brought in Patrick Nolan, a colleague at the University of South Carolina. As a junior author, Nolan's role in *Human Societies* gradually expanded as Lenski began to retire from academic life. In 1992, shortly after his wife's death, Lenski left Chapel Hill. In 1996 he married Ann Blalock, a policy evaluation researcher and they now both live in Washington state where he continues work on new editions of *Human Societies* as well as other writing projects in evolutionary sociology.

Lenski's sociology developed in conjunction with his teaching. Arriving as a young instructor at the University of Michigan in 1950, Lenski was assigned to teach four introductory sociology courses. "This proved to be an extraordinarily frustrating experience, since it was impossible to provide students with a meaningfully integrated and cumulative view of sociology when building on a functionalist foundation." His best students would complain of the fragmentation, the jargon, and the disconnected elements of the course. After some years of this he read Walter Goldschmidt's *Man's Way: A Preface to the Understanding of Human Society*. In this book, Goldschmidt, an anthropologist, presented the outlines of a more modern version of a social evolutionary perspective. Unlike the older perspectives of Spencer and Sumner, Goldschmidt focused much more attention on subsistence technology. For Lenski, this evolutionary perspective suggested ways in which he could pull together the disparate pieces of his introductory course "into a coherent and provocative whole." This was to eventually lead to *Human Societies* in 1970. Since its initial publication, *Human Societies* has provided this holistic alternative for thousands of sociology students.

NOTES

1. While Lenski is well-known in the field for writing several editions of *Human Societies: An Introduction to Macrosociology*, this success has probably caused him to be very underrated as a social theorist—academics do not accord much prestige to such efforts. Nevertheless, he constructs and systematically tests a comprehensive theory in these works, each edition refining the theory and providing further tests of its efficacy. The recent publication of *Ecological-Evolutionary Theory: Principles and Applications* (2005) should force many social scientists to reassess his status.

2. The first of these was written by Lenski alone in 1970. The 6th edition I refer to in this chapter was published in 1991. I use this because it presents a more mature version of ecological-evolutionary theory and because it is one of the last in which Gerhard was the first author. It is also the latest edition that happened to be on my bookshelf.

3. This view of a loose system in which multiple functions and dysfunctions become possible is, of course, consistent with structural functional theory. While Lenski is not a functionalist, like the other macro theorists in this volume he has been influenced by functional theory. By viewing societies as sociocultural *systems*, it is natural to view the various parts of these systems as functionally related to each other and to the whole. By focusing on social systems as "loose," Lenski is allowing for dysfunctions as well as conflict within. Functionalism is, however, only a small part of the ecological-evolutionary paradigm (see Lenski, 2005, pp.10–11).

4. The "class consciousness" concept is from Karl Marx.

5. The multidimensional view of stratification led Lenski to hypothesize early in his career about a condition called "status inconsistency." According to Lenski an individual who has widely dissimilar rankings on different stratification dimensions—one who ranks high on one dimension and low on others—"is subjected to certain pressures which are not felt (at least in the same degree) by individuals with a more crystallized status." This pressure is produced because an individual has a vested interest in thinking of the self in terms of that status or rank which is the highest, and others have a vested interest in treating that person in terms of his or her lower rank. This creates considerable stress for people of inconsistent status and may lead them to oppose the social order (Lenski, 1954). Lenski (1966) illustrates his concept with an example of a black doctor and a white laborer. "The former, motivated by self-interest, will strive to establish the relation on the basis of occupation (or perhaps education or wealth), while the later, similarly motivated, will strive to establish the relation on the basis of race. Since each regards his own point of view as right and proper ... one, or both, are likely to be frustrated, and probably angered by the experience" (p. 87). Because they are likely to have access to important resources (such as wealth or education), it is the status inconsistent, Lenski believes, who provide the leadership in revolutionary and reform movements.

6. Perhaps a better example is given by Stephen J. Gould in his discussion of the typewriter (and now computer) keyboard. Gould uses the keyboard to illustrate the idea that previous adaptation is an impediment to further change in natural evolution (yet another parallel between natural and social evolution). The layout of the standard keyboard, called "Qwerty" (look at the letters above left "home row") was originally devised to slow the typist down because early typewriters were subject to jamming if the typist went too fast. Subsequent developments lifted this mechanical limitation, and new keyboards were developed that placed the most frequently used letters in more convenient places and allowed even the best typists to substantially increase their typing speed. However, people had already committed to Qwerty, thousands of typewriters were already in existence, millions had been trained in the use of the Qwerty system. Consequently, because of past adaptations, the innovation never became widespread, an inferior (and less well adapted) typing system prevailed (Gould, 1996).

7. I was struck upon first reading *Guns, Germs, and Steel* by Jared Diamond with how consistent the book was with ecological-evolutionary theory, though there is little reference at all to anthropological or sociological literature. Lenski remarks on this in his 2005 work as well: "Finally, for those who desire additional tests of ecological-evolutionary theory, I strongly recommend Jared Diamond's excellent volume, *Guns, Germs, and Steel: The Fates of Human Societies.* Although Diamond does not label his analysis as ecological and evolutionary, and though there are some differences in his perspective, these differences are not major. Thus, most of the chapters in *Guns, Germs, and Steel* provide valuable further tests of the principles on which ecological-evolutionary theory is based" (Lenski, 2005, p. 145).

8. Different social scientists may use different classification schemes, and there are other types of societies that could be identified that are not included on this chart. Though not as widespread, for example, there are pastoral, fishing, and maritime societies that have adapted to specific environments. It is interesting to note that most social scientists as well as many lay-people favor some such scheme of classifying societies based on their mode of production. In discussing international relations, it is helpful to identify whether a society is industrial, or agrarian, as well as how developed it is within either of the categories. By referring to societies as such there is an implicit recognition that subsistence technology is central in understanding the institutions, attitudes, and beliefs within those societies.

9. Consider the changes that have occurred in advanced industrial societies with the aging of the population.

10. In *Human Societies*, Lenski's theory becomes more evolutionary and broader in focus, and then, over succeeding editions, his theory is continually tested and refined through the examination of these same societal types.

11. As a graduate student I was very impressed. Until reading Lenski's *Power and Privilege*, I had never encountered a book in which the author's central hypothesis was rejected by the evidence. He then goes on to thoroughly explore the reasons behind this rejection. I am still impressed.

12. Lenski ruefully admits this in his 2005 work in which he remarks on the clever nature of these "golden rubles" in disguising the true amount of inequality from social scientists (2005, pp. 217–218).

13. Lenski found that Agrarian elites were collecting up to 50 percent of all income (1966, p. 309).

14. Ideology that seeks to limit welfare to the needy does not seem to apply to wealthfare for our more prominent citizens. As countless observers have pointed out, the amount of money and government services that go to our wealthiest citizens, both direct and indirect (in the form of tax breaks), dwarfs the amount that is spent on welfare for the poor.

15. The average CEO made 42 times the average hourly worker's pay in 1980. In 1990 they made 85 times more, in 2000 531 times more. Due to the recession of 2001, however, their pay was only 411 times as much. In 2003 the average CEO of a major company made $9.2 million in total compensation.

The pay of CEOs in most other nations are well below these levels. Source: AFL-CIO Website on Executive Pay Watch http://www.aflcio.org /corporateamerica/paywatch/

16. This section is based on personal correspondence I had with Professor Lenski in the fall of 2003.

5

Meta-Analysis

In the 1970s, social science "meta-analysis," or comparing, contrasting, and synthesizing several studies on a single subject, was all the rage. Such a meta-analysis of the four theories presented in this volume might provide some further insights to advance our understanding of social order and change.

Both Lenski and Harris are in agreement that population and production variables in interaction with the environment, are the primary determinants of the rest of the sociocultural system. Harris tends to take a pretty hard causal line on this, insisting theoretically on the primacy of the infrastructure, though softening that line in subsequent empirical analyses and allowing that such structural factors as capitalist organization and bureaucracy as well as superstructural ideologies play some feedback role in system stability and change. His theoretical focus, however, is of the primacy of the infrastructure. Lenski, seeking to integrate and synthesize an incredible variety of theories, explicitly allows that structures and ideologies play a significant though secondary role. Making a virtue of keeping his theory open, however, he does run the danger of allowing it to "degenerate into a mushy, formless eclecticism (Lenski, 2005, p. 138).

Another difference between the two theories is in the treatment of the influence of the sociocultural environment on a society. Again, Lenski treats this more explicitly, giving it equal footing with the natural environment itself. Diffusion from other societies through social contact is one of the most frequent sources of sociocultural innovation and change. Harris does not treat diffusion explicitly in the theory of cultural materialism. In his analyses of societies he seeks to control for such social influences. Harris is far more concerned with "pristine" changes, changes such as the rise of capitalism or agriculture brought about in societies that have not acquired these innovations from other sociocultural systems. His central question is "how have infrastructural/environmental relations led to these innovations"? Clearly Harris is aware that diffusion is far more common than innovation, but it is not

his focus, nor is his theory equipped to deal with it well.[1] Ecological-
evolutionary theory is far more inclusive and explicitly multicausal
than cultural materialism, though they clearly share a strong ecological-
materialist base.

Mills and Wallerstein, on the other hand, focus strongly on the
structural variables of bureaucracy and capitalism. Mills allows that the
"master trend" of our time may well be industrialization, but his primary concern is with the effects that these new production technologies
have upon structures and upon people. Taking his cue from Weber,
Mills expresses grave reservations about the growth of corporate, government, and military bureaucracy and the subsequent rationalization of
social life.[2] Apart from the process of rationalization and bureaucratization, Mills saw capitalism as a force in-and-of-itself within sociocultural systems.[3] Wallerstein's emphasis, of course, is on the capitalist
world-system and the impact this system has on the international division of labor and relations between nation states. In accordance with his
insistence that the only true social systems are world-systems, Wallerstein has little focus on the effects of capitalism within the nation state
itself. In his analyses of the rise and fall of capitalism, hegemony, and
other world-systems processes he frequently cites materialistic factors
such as depletion, pollution, technological intensification, and population, as well as such structural factors as government and capitalist enterprises. However, Wallerstein's world-systems analysis is not a theory; it is rather an insistence that social scientists consider the world-
system context when studying social organizations and their impact on
human behavior. While he employs materialist and structural factors
frequently in his analysis, there is little explicit theoretical development
of materialist, structural, or idealist perspectives.

THE RISE OF CAPITALISM

The common as well as divergent emphases and strategies of the four
theorists can clearly be seen with reference to their treatment of the rise
of Western capitalism and the establishment of the modern world. Why
did capitalism arise in Western Europe? Why at the end of the Middle
Ages? Why the economic and political dominance of the West? These
are very famous questions. Both Marx and Weber attempted to answer
them. Marx's explanation rested on his concept of class struggle between the lords and the rising bourgeoisie of the towns. Weber's on the
rise of the "Protestant Ethic." Modern theorists such as Mills, Harris,
Wallerstein, and Lenski, as well as others not dealt with directly in this

book have continued the debate. As will be seen, the areas of agreement between the four theorists in this book are actually substantial.

As a student of Max Weber, C. Wright Mills was committed to a multicausal view of sociocultural stability and change. In the interpretation of Gerth and Mills, Weber's Protestant ethic hypothesis was merely an attempt to "round out" Marx's economic materialism. "As a view of world history, Marxism seemed to him an untenable monocausal theory and thus prejudicial to an adequate reconstruction of social and historical connections" (Gerth and Mills, 1946/1965, pp. 46-47). Accordingly, both Weber and Mills see the Protestant ethic as providing theological justification and motivation for behaviors that advanced the accumulation of capital.

In illustrating their concept of a "coincidence of orders," in which they claim that such institutional coincidence is fairly common, Gerth and Mills (1953, pp. 360–363) summarize the thesis that Calvinism, with a view of an inscrutable God predestining only a few for salvation, encouraged behavior favorable to capital accumulation. In this review they note that the Puritans came to view everyday behavior as a good indicator—though not a guarantee—that a particular person was predestined for salvation. To demonstrate to your fellows that you were among the elect, you disciplined yourself through work as "an ascetic exercise." By demonstrating to your fellows this discipline through hard work and thrift, you were allowed membership (through adult baptism) into the sect. The accumulation of wealth rather than its consumption became the mark of good Christian stewardship, this accumulated capital to be reinvested in business for intensifying production. This allowed the Puritan entrepreneur to employ others—extending to them the opportunities to prove themselves worthy to their fellows as well. Finally, membership in the sect gave the rising capitalist some cushion in economic hard times. "This relevance of sect membership for credit, based upon religiously trained character, facilitates economic ascent" (Gerth and Mills, 1953, p. 361). Thus, Gerth and Mills conclude, the new religious asceticism provides religious motive for the never-ending accumulation of capital.

As they are committed to the principles of system and multicausality, however, Gerth and Mills take pains to point out that they are talking of *only* one strand in the causal order. They go on to write of the role of religious ideas in the larger scheme:

> The ramifications of Puritanism, and hence of the primarily religious phenomenon, *fed into* the great economic transition from feudalism to modern industrial capitalism. The decline of the guild system and its restraints on competition, the technological and organizational ad-

vances of the workshop, were reinforced by the migration of perse-
cuted Protestant minorities who established themselves outside urban
jurisdictions. ...The numerous technological, monetary, and organizational changes in the age of discoveries, and changes in trade
routes from the Mediterranean to the Atlantic, *found an area of coin-
ciding changes* in religion, in personality formation, and in new religiously motivated ways of playing the crucial roles instrumental in the
emergence of modern industrial capitalism. (1953, p. 362, emphasis
added)

Like Weber, Mills believes in multicausality, in a sociocultural system
in which material conditions, structures, and ideas are reciprocally related, sometimes by design, sometimes by fortuitous coincidence. In
other writings Mills makes clear that he gives considerably more
weight to material and structural factors, but he remains strongly committed to the interrelations between the three factors.

The question Harris poses (or the "riddle," if you will), is why the
economic system of capitalism develops in Europe precisely when it
did? Why didn't it develop independently in other cultures and in other
times?[4] To answer this question, Harris proposes that we first look at
the collapse of European feudalism, the economic system that capitalism replaced. Harris first notes that many explanations rely on rising
trade. The idea is that as manufacture and trade gradually increased in
the tenth and eleventh centuries, the wealth of the merchant class, as
well as the constant search for profit undermined feudal relations (Harris, 1977, pp. 256–257; Harris, 1999, pp. 169–170). But, Harris points
out, there is nothing in the feudal system that is hostile to trade. The
towns with their resident artisans and merchants were an integral part
of feudal life, facilitating trade and manufacture and supplying the
manor with goods and services that it could not produce itself. Nor
were the feudal lords opposed to the market or the making of a profit. It
was only after some 500 years of this symbiotic relationship that capitalism begins to displace feudalism (Harris, 1977, pp. 256–257).

Harris believes the transition from feudalism to capitalism was
rooted in the failure of feudalism to provide for a rise in the population
level in Europe (Harris, 1977, p. 257; 1999, pp. 166–167). This rise in
population was met with the intensification of agriculture, soil depletion, cutting of forests, and putting more marginal land into production
(Harris, 1999, p. 166). As population density rose, agricultural efficiencies declined for the lord of the manor as well. In response, the lords
would take some of their lands out of food production to raise sheep for
wool, thus supplementing their income. This, of course, reduced the
amount of land available for peasants and their crops and caused many

to leave the manor for the towns. As in all systems of declining effi- ciencies, attempts were made to intensify production on the remaining land, such as new seed varieties, plowing-in ash in the fields, and other techniques to increase yields per acre. However, when successful, these innovations were met with further population increases.

To support his hypothesis, Harris points to several indicators of hard times at the end of the feudal era. First, the price of wheat "almost trebled between the late twelfth and early fourteenth century at the same time that English exports of wool rose by 40 percent. A rise in grain prices meant that families who lacked sufficient lands to feed themselves were pushed down close to or below the pauperization threshold" (1977, pp. 257–258). The second indicator of hard times is the rise in the number of infanticides. For various reasons the practice of infanticide is selectively practiced on female infants.[5] While the practice is hidden in most cultures, a good secondary indicator that it is being widely practiced is to look at the adolescent sex ratio of boys to girls. Harris reports that the "ratio rose to a peak of 130:100 between 1250 and 1358, and remained drastically imbalanced for another cen- tury" (Harris, 1977, p. 258).

A final indicator of hard times at the end of the feudal era in Europe is the arrival in 1348 of the plague. Harris estimates that the "Black Death" killed between one-quarter and one-half of the European population. He posits that the reason the mortality rate was so high was because of malnutrition, which lowers resistance to disease in general. Further contributing demographic causes of the plague were the move- ment of a larger percentage of the population to towns and the conse- quent increase in overall density of the population (Harris, 1977, p. 259; Harris, 1999, p. 166). The ensuing turmoil in Europe following the plague—peasant revolts, the Reformation, the Inquisition, and the seemingly endless wars—indicates a period of intense political, eco- nomic, and social unrest (Harris, 1977, p. 259).

But after the depopulation caused by the Black Death, Harris asks, why didn't the society settle back into the feudal system? Because, he answers, "labor shortages after 1350 merely added another set of forces to those that were corroding the old manorial system and hastening the development of wage labor, commerce, and entrepreneurship" (Harris, 1999, pp. 166–167). People make productive and reproductive deci- sions based on costs and benefits. To maximize their political and eco- nomic interests, the lords enclosed more lands in order to raise more sheep and manufacture more woolen cloth. Because of the labor short- ages, it was in the interests of the peasants to sell their labor rather than work the marginal lands available to them at the manor (Harris, 1977, pp. 261–262).

But there is another factor that allowed the values and interests of merchants and manufacturers to become dominant in Europe.[6] In many previous societies the interests of merchants were kept in check by elites whose wealth was based on land. China, Harris points out, independently developed many of the features of capitalist society— markets for agricultural products and manufactured goods, banks, an emerging merchant class. But these elements were always subordinate to the Chinese bureaucracy, and success depended on the arbitrary and capricious support of the state (Harris, 1977, pp. 262–263).[7] In contrast, European societies were never so centralized, rulers were never so absolute.

Citing Karl Wittfogel, Harris points out that Chinese agriculture depends on dams and complex irrigation systems, systems that are built and maintained through centralized authority. Wittfogel calls these "hydraulic societies." They arise in river valleys; they tend to be very stable. When their populations inevitably run up against environmental limits they too experience population collapse. But after the crash, restoration of the irrigation system remains the priority of both elite and commoner. As a result, these societies were remarkably stable; they lasted for hundreds if not thousands of years.

European agriculture, on the other hand, is dependent on rainfall. The benefits of centralization are few, competing centers of power develop. At one time Harris estimates that there were as many as a thousand different feudal states in Europe. Within these states were nobility, an often independent church, and the free guilds, independent towns and cities (Harris, 1999, p. 173). While the rulers of Europe claimed absolute authority, their power was always somewhat limited by these competing centers of power (Harris, 1977, p. 264). Consequently, the power of the rulers to confiscate profits was minimal; though the opportunity for alliance between merchants and kings, or for merchants and nobility to be allied against the ruler, were substantial indeed.[8]

Wallerstein's analysis of the origins of capitalism is a materialist explanation that differs only a little in the details as given by Harris. According to Wallerstein, capitalism arose in Western Europe in the "long-sixteenth century"[9] as a solution to the crisis of feudalism. European feudalism, Wallerstein argues, should be seen as an economic system based on hundreds of small manor-based production units in which most of the surplus was taken by the landlords. These landlords had noble status and controlled property and legal relations (Wallerstein, 1974, p. 18). Through this system both productivity and population gradually increased through the centuries of the Middle Ages. Since much of the surplus was of foodstuffs that could not be consumed by the nobility alone, the expansion of trade was very much a part of the feudal system as well (Wallerstein, 1974, pp. 18–20).

The crisis of feudalism begins in the fourteenth century as the expansion of population, productivity, and trade was halted by a combination of factors. First, Wallerstein cites the primary factor as declining efficiencies due to limitations in technology. There were no new lands to bring into cultivation, increases in productivity of the land were no longer possible given the level of technological development (Wallerstein, 1974, p. 37). Wallerstein claims that "diminishing returns" on stable technology became the rule. There were no structural motivations for technological innovation; peasants had no incentive to develop new technology to increase their productivity since the lords took the bulk of the surplus, and lords had no knowledge of the land or of technology to innovate themselves. "While productivity remained stable (or even possibly declined as a result of soil exhaustion) because of the absence of structure motivation for technological advance, the burden to be borne by the producers of the surplus had been constantly expanding because of the growing size and level of expenditure of the ruling class. There was no more to be squeezed out" (Wallerstein, 1974, p. 37). Another explanation given credence by Wallerstein is a change in climate in Europe, the "little Ice Age." This climate change had impact on the productivity of the land and thus the amount of surplus that could be expropriated. It is the combination of these factors, Wallerstein argues, which led to the crisis of feudalism—a geographical contraction from areas previously cultivated, a decline in population, and a decline in trade (and probably productivity) (Wallerstein, 1974, p. 37).

For Wallerstein the crisis of feudalism has to be due to a multiplicity of material and structural factors, because it is only through the buildup of immense pressure that such enormous social change could occur. The crisis of feudalism was not solved by any central agency or political unit in Europe acting in a purposeful manner to establish capitalism. Rather, the capitalist economic system evolved as the result of the actions of "groups of men acting in terms of their immediate interests" (Wallerstein, 1974, p. 51). It is at this point that Wallerstein diverges from more traditional social science—not in the analysis of its emergence, but rather in what it was that emerged.

What was in their immediate interests was the establishment of a world-economy based on an extremely unequal division of labor between European states and the rest of the system. Also in their interest was the institution of strong European states that had the political and military will to enforce this inequality. And finally, it was in their interests to have the great masses of workers around the world produce not only profit for their enterprises but also taxes for governments to be used in maintaining the world-system (Wallerstein, 1974, pp. 356–357). But it is not simply the interests of elites that have to be taken into account in the creation of the modern world. The peasants, workers, serfs, natives, the exploited of all types also have a hand in the creation, maintenance, and change within the system (Wallerstein, 1974, p. 357). Like Marx, it is this conflict between the exploiters and the exploited that gives the system much of its dynamism. "The mark of the modern world is the imagination of its profiteers and the counter-assertiveness of the oppressed. Exploitation and the refusal to accept exploitation as either inevitable or just constitute the continuing antimony of the modern era, joined together in a dialectic which has far from reached its climax in the twentieth century" (Wallerstein, 1974, p. 357).

Lenski (1991, 2005) also seeks to explain the rise of capitalism and western European economic dominance beginning in the sixteenth century. He correctly points out that Western Europe at this time had no inherent advantages in geography, being on one end of the Eurasian continent. Nor was it blessed with abundant natural resources—in fact, much of the arable land was already under cultivation; many of its forests already cut down. What was it about Western European societies that gave it the edge in economic development? Lenski answers that there was one significant factor indeed, the discovery and eventual settlement of the New World. This gave Western European societies access and control over vast resources and quickly transformed their economies, and allowed them to play a dominant role in the developing world economy (Lenski, 2005, p. 175). The discovery and exploitation of the New World gave elites in Western European societies access to abundant natural resources which they rapidly converted to unprecedented wealth.

The exploration and subsequent exploitation of the New World was enabled by technological developments (much of it through diffusion from other Eurasian societies) in ship design and building, navigation techniques such as the compass, as well as gunpowder, and the printing press. It was technological innovation that was at the root of discoveries, not changes in structures or developments in ideology. Lenski summarizes his theory:

> the basic causal sequence appears to have been initiated by (1) advances in the technologies of navigation and water transportation beginning late in the twelfth century, which stimulated the many voy-

ages of exploration in the fifteenth century and made the discovery of the New World possible, and (2) subsequent advances in military technology, in combination with the tremendous impact of diseases brought to the Americas by Europeans, which made the conquest of these two vast continents possible; (3) this, in turn, provided western European societies with a wealth of new resources that (4) vastly increased the money supply, stimulated trade and commerce, led to the rapid expansion of markets, and strengthened the merchant class while weakening the old landed aristocracy, thus (5) laying a foundation for revolutionary advances in agricultural and industrial technology in the eighteenth, nineteenth, and twentieth centuries, which (6), in combination with the wealth of resources controlled by Western societies, became the basis of their vastly expanded power, prestige, and wealth in the late nineteenth and twentieth centuries. (Lenski 2005, p. 181)

Lenski does not believe he has developed an exhaustive theory of the rise of the West; he concedes that structural and ideological factors will also enter into any thorough investigation, but such forces, in Lenski's view, are secondary in explaining sociocultural stability and change.[10]

EXCURSUS: THE GROWTH OF BUREAUCRACY

Before concluding I wish to examine the material, structural and idealist causes (that is, perform a systems analysis) of the rise to dominance of that other great structural innovation of modern society, bureaucratic organization. As detailed by numerous social scientists in this volume and elsewhere, bureaucracy, independent of economic and political institutions, is a dominant social force in industrial and hyperindustrial societies. Perhaps the best way of looking at bureaucracy is as a social technology; it is the detailed division of labor applied to human organization. Recall that according to Weber, characteristics associated with bureaucracy include: (1) a highly specialized division of labor; (2) a hierarchy of authority, (3) written rules of conduct, (4) impersonality, (5) advancement within the organization based on expertise, and (5) efficiency in the attainment of institutional goals. Bureaucracy is a social technology used by governments, capitalists, and other groups to more efficiently attain their goals. A healthy bureaucracy is always in the process of "bureaucratization." The bureaucratization process refers to the changes within organizations toward greater rationality, that is, improved operating efficiency and more effective attainment of common goals. While the spur to accumulate capital may keep corporate bureaucracy somewhat leaner and more efficient,[11] bureaucratization pervades nearly all aspects of modern life including government (all levels), voluntary organizations, all types of education, medicine, sports, and even crime.[12]

There are at least seven characteristics of the sociocultural system that promote the growth of bureaucracy. Three of these characteristics are of the infrastructure: the intensification of industrial mode of production; population growth; and the adoption of new technologies of communications, transportation, and coordination. Two are structural characteristics: the decline of primary groups and the "organizational imperative." And finally, two are superstructural characteristics: the decline of the social bond and the rationalization process itself.

One of the fundamental reasons behind the emergence and growth of bureaucracies is that they enable large-scale tasks to be performed. The use of energy sources other than human and animal power, the growth of mass production, and the increase in job specialization has led to greater needs for coordination of these diverse activities. A modern automobile-manufacturing corporation, for example, must coordinate the activities of thousands of employees, suppliers, financiers, and dealers around the globe. More complex technologies and markets require rational social organization for coordination, control, and regulation of these activities.

The growth of population has a similar impact on the bureaucratization process. Greater numbers of people require rational social organization for the coordination, control, and regulation of their activities. The world has experienced exponential growth in population over the last two centuries; while slowing in recent decades, this growth is continuing. In addition, industrial societies of the north are gaining in population through immigration—a population that requires closer monitoring and control than native population growth.

Thus, it has been necessary to control and supervise large masses of people in an effort to deal more efficiently with their needs and problems, as well as to provide increasing numbers of people with employment opportunities. Bureaucracies meet these kinds of demands. As population has increased, formal organizations have proliferated and grown to solve problems of adapting to the environment (government and corporations), handling survival needs (sanitation and food production), and providing social services (welfare and medical care).

A third infrastructural factor promoting the proliferation and growth of bureaucracies is the new communication and transportation technologies. Many of these technologies were foreseen by Mills, but Wallerstein also comments on how the new technologies enable the centralization and growth of the world capitalist system itself. "It should however be noted that the size of a world-economy is a function of the state of technology, and in particular of the possibilities of transport and communication within its bounds" (1974, p. 349).

A fourth factor behind the growth of bureaucracies is a structural cause, the decline in the size, influence, and importance of primary group organization. Hyperindustrial society requires an extremely mobile population. Because of the detailed division of labor, people are required to move from one end of the country to the other in order to engage in their occupations. Uneven growth also causes increases in geographic mobility. In addition, the specialized division of labor requires diverse educational and training organizations—it would not do to have a brain surgeon trained at her father's knee. Finally, bureaucratic-industrial society requires social mobility as well. This has had the effect of weakening many traditional groups such as the family and the community. In a more traditional society, these groups provide many services to the individual—child care, social security, financial aid, education, social control, medical care, counseling, and a wealth of other services. With the decline of primary groups, many secondary organizations have arisen in hyperindustrial society to provide services that used to be performed by these groups.

The rise of bureaucracy, then, is in large part an effort to deal with the breakdown of traditional ways of organizing social life. What the family, community, ethnic groups, friendship network, and church once did, private corporations and government now attempt to do. While traditional institutions provided aid and services on the basis of group ties, bureaucracies provide aid and services through contractual legal relationships. While many conservatives argue that it is the expansion of bureaucratic power itself that weakens primary groups, such an argument confuses cause and effect. The traditional ways broke down because of infrastructural intensification—we cannot solve our problems simply by willing traditional families, communities, and values back into existence.

A fifth characteristic that promotes the growth of bureaucracy is called the "organizational imperative." The creation of bureaucracies themselves has often required the creation of other bureaucracies to supervise, control, or deal with them. Government bureaucracies often mediate the struggles between companies or regulate their behavior so that they cannot exploit the powerless or the environment. In the name of education, welfare, taxation, safety, health, and the environment, state bureaucratic power has grown to protect individuals and groups from being exploited by corporations and other secondary organizations. Unions are another example of a bureaucratic organization that arose to give voice to individual workers who were dealing with large-scale organizations. Many groups have organized to deal on a more equal basis with already established state and corporate bureaucracies.

A sixth factor behind the bureaucratization process is the rise of individualism and the decline of the social bond and trust in society. This has consequences both within the organization and in the relations between various organizations. Within the organization the decline is directly responsible for the need to regulate and monitor employees and clients. Bureaucracies are based on contractual self-interested relationships in which human ties of loyalty, love, and commitment have few legitimate outlets of expression. The sheer size of these organizations, the multiple levels of authority, as well as the detailed division of labor promote distrust and the need to monitor the performance of those lower in the hierarchy. Braverman (1974/1998, p. 210) comments on how the internal record keeping of such organizations is structured around the assumption that their employees are dishonest, lazy, or in some way disloyal. The modern organization therefore engages in constant monitoring of employees, documentation, and formal assessment of their performance. The shuffling of forms and reports that communicate information and decisions up and down the hierarchy augments this continual monitoring and assessment of employee performance.

The lack of trust and social bond is also evident in the relations between organizations. The fact that these institutions are designed to efficiently achieve limited goals without regard to broader sociocultural values—whether that goal is profit, gathering intelligence, or defending the nation—makes these institutions particularly prone to offensive behavior. Such institutions must closely monitor and document their dealings with one another. Braverman (1974/1998) points out that corporations must presume that their transactions with one another are fundamentally dishonest, each must painstakingly document each transaction to prevent fraudulence by the other. In addition, since the corporation must file financial statements for the purpose of luring investors and borrowing from banks, this necessitates an independent audit to certify the truth and accuracy of their books. All this necessitates yet more clerical work and duplicate records. "And to this may be added much of the work of government regulatory and tax offices which deal with the same material from still other standpoints" (pp. 209–210).

This lack of trust does not just exist within and between corporations and government, but within and between all organizations and their dealings with each other. Institutions of higher education, for example, must fill out voluminous reports on enrollments, educational goals, assessment of student learning, and graduate placement to state educational bureaucracies as well as to regional accreditation agencies. Without proper monitoring (and coordination), it is feared, there is no telling what universities and colleges may teach our children. Criminal justice agencies, medical treatment facilities, social service agencies, and others all face similar "accountability" standards to governments, regulatory agencies, and third-party payers. In the not too distant past, these agencies were free to practice (and malpractice) without this type of monitoring—there was a certain amount of credit and trust put in professionalism and local control. This is no longer true. As a result of growth in numbers, complexity, individualism, and the detailed division of labor the consequent loss of trust and social bond has lead to a rise in the number of administrators and their ubiquitous bureaucratic red tape. This has meant the proliferation of reports, forms, accreditations, receipts (in triplicate), and greater detailed electronic and paper record keeping and retrieval. It is this aspect of bureaucracy that is primarily responsible for its reputation as both inefficient and wasteful, and bureaucrats as pushing paper for a living.

Finally, the rationalization process has also promoted the growth of bureaucracies. Bureaucracies are built on the principles of efficiency and calculability. The rationalization process refers to a set of norms and values that increasingly dominate industrial society. It is a habit of thought involving a persistent questioning of the adequacy of means to ends and a constant search for more adequate means. The result is a society that is constantly questioning traditional ways, devising more rational ways to achieve desired ends. Rationalization is the integrating mechanism of modern social life, replacing more traditional institutions and values that are in increasing conflict with the intensifying infrastructure. The rationalization of superstructure provides positive feedback for the further bureaucratization of structure, both of which provide positive feedback for the further intensification of infrastructure.

CONCLUSION

In addition to developing a comprehensive macro theory rooted in the classical tradition, each of the theorists reviewed in this volume rejected the narrow specialization of our day and explicitly argued that we must abandon the arbitrary and capricious boundaries between the social science disciplines. Each of these theorists read widely and drew heavily from history, anthropology, sociology, economics, and political science, as well as current world affairs. Like the founders of the social sciences themselves, each has attempted to contribute to a general understanding of the human condition. This, in my opinion, is the primary function of the social sciences within the university and within the broader sociocultural system. It is an essential part of the examined life.

NOTES

1. In a related vein, it is interesting to note the role that bureaucracy plays in Harris's analysis of modern American society in *America Now* (1981), though his theory is not well equipped to deal with the phenomena. As a cultural anthropologist, Harris is very concerned with describing/explaining sociocultural practices and beliefs. In other words, his focus is almost exclusively on structures and superstructures as dependent variables—to be explained by infrastructural processes. While Harris frequently argues that structures and superstructures interact with infrastructural processes, his theory has a difficult time generalizing these interactions. In *Industrializing America* (1999, pp. 9–28) I present a sociological revision of cultural materialism to address these problems.

2. Having served within educational bureaucracies for over twenty-five years now, I share his concerns.

3. This view can clearly be seen in the following quote: "Above all, the privately incorporated economy must be made over into a publicly responsible economy. I am aware of the magnitude of this task, but either we take democracy seriously or we do not. This corporate economy, as it is now constituted, is an undemocratic growth within the formal democracy of the United States" (Mills, 1958, pp. 123–124).

4. Actually, Harris's 1999 analysis concedes that capitalism arises independently in Japan about 200 years after its European development. The reason for its emergence there, Harris concludes, are the same as the reasons for its emergence in Europe.

5. See Harris's "Murders in Eden" which appears in *Cannibals and Kings: The Origins of Cultures*, pp. 11–25.

6. Markets and production for profit have probably existed since the beginnings of human history. The central question of the rise of capitalism is not its origins but rather its ascendance to dominance in the affairs of sociocultural systems.

7. Note that China's state bureaucracy is a structural factor.

8. Again, structural and superstructural factors.

9. The long sixteenth century refers to the period 1450 to 1640 in which the capitalist world-economy was established (1974, p. 67).

10. Lenski does not think very highly of the Protestant ethic hypothesis. At best, he believes, it is but a contributing factor in explaining the rise of the West (2005, pp. 180–181). As one who admires Weber above all other social scientists, I am in full agreement. While beliefs and values often reinforce or

strengthen behavior, the evidence for the Protestant ethic as a great stimulus to capital accumulation appears to be pretty weak. Weber still rules.

11. This would be true if there is competition for a given market. In markets characterized by monopoly or oligopoly, Harris points out, there is no economic spur to keep bureaucracies lean.

12. An exception to the process in the United States is labor. Since the 1950s, labor organizations (and thus bureaucracies) have been in sharp decline in terms of membership and power. Much of this decline can be directly attributable to the rise of corporate power in relation to labor and in the corporations influence on government.

References

Adams, Phoebe. 1968, September. "The Rise of Anthropological Theory" (book review). *Atlantic Monthly* 222 (3): 134.

Beidelman, Thomas O. 1980. "Cultural Materialism: The Struggle for a Science of Culture" (book review). *American Journal of Sociology:* 1245–1247.

Bierstedt, Robert. 1956, December. "*The Power Elite* by C. Wright Mills" (book review). *Political Science Quarterly* 71(4).

Braverman, Harry. 1974. *Labor and Monopoly Capital: The Degradation of Work in the Twentieth Century.* New York: Monthly Review Press.

Burns, Allan. 2001, "Marvin Harris Making an Impact in Mozambique and Brazil" (obituary). *Guardian,* December 13.

Diamond, Jared. 1997. *Guns, Germs, and Steel: The Fates of Human Societies.* New York: W. W. Norton.

Dye, Thomas. 2000. *Who's Running America? The Clinton Years.* 6th ed. Upper Saddle River, NJ: Prentice Hall.

Dye, Thomas. 2002. *Who's Running America? The Bush Restoration.* 7th ed. Upper Saddle River, NJ: Prentice Hall.

Elwell, Frank W. 1992. *The Evolution of the Future.* New York: Praeger.

Elwell, Frank W. 1999. *Industrializing America: Understanding Contemporary Society through Classical Sociological Analysis.* New York: Praeger.

Elwell, Frank W. 2001. *A Commentary on Malthus' 1798 Essay on Population as Social Theory.* Lewiston, ME: Edwin Mellen Press.

Ferguson, R. Brian. 1995. "Infrastructural Determinism." In *Science, Materialism, and the Study of Culture,* edited by Martin F. Murphy and Maxine Margolis. Gainesville: University of Florida Press.

Form, William. 1995. "Mills at Maryland." *American Sociologist* 26(3).

Gerth, Hans H., and C. Wright Mills. 1946/1965. *From Max Weber: Essays in Sociology.* New York: Oxford University Press.

Gerth, Hans H., and C. Wright Mills. 1953. *Character and Social Structure: The Psychology of Social Institutions.* New York: Harcourt, Brace.

Gould, Stephen Jay. 1991. *Bully for Brontosaurus: Reflections in Natural History.* New York: W. W. Norton.

Gould, Stephen Jay. 1996. *Full House: The Spread of Excellence from Plato to Darwin.* New York: Three Rivers Press.

Harris, Marvin. 1968. *The Rise of Anthropological Theory.* New York: Crowell.

Harris, Marvin. 1971. *Culture, Man, and Nature: An Introduction to General Anthropology.* New York: Crowell.

Harris, Marvin. 1974. *Cows, Pigs, Wars, and Witches: The Riddles of Culture.* New York: Random House.

Harris, Marvin. 1977. *Cannibals and Kings*. New York: Vintage Books.

Harris, Marvin. 1979. *Cultural Materialism*. New York: Random House.

Harris, Marvin. 1981. *America Now: The Anthropology of a Changing Culture*. New York: Simon and Schuster.

Harris, Marvin. 1989. *Our Kind: Who We Are, Where We Came From, and Where We Are Going*. New York: HarperCollins.

Harris, Marvin. 1998. *Theories of Culture in Postmodern Times*. Walnut Creek, CA: AltaMira Press.

Horowitz, Irving. L. 1983. *C. Wright Mills: An American Utopian*. New York: Free Press.

Judas, John B. 2001, March. "Grist for Mills." *Texas Monthly* 29(3).

Kent, Mary M., and Mark Mather. 2002, December. "What Drives U.S. Population Growth?" *Population Bulletin* 57.

Kuhn, Thomas. 1962/1996. *The Structure of Scientific Revolutions*. 3rd ed. Chicago: University of Chicago Press.

Kumar, Krishan. 1978. *Prophecy and Progress*. New York: Penguin.

Lenski, Gerhard E. 1954. "Status Crystallization: A Non-Vertical Dimension of Social Status," *American Sociological Review* 19: 404–413.

Lenski, Gerhard E. 1966. *Power and Privilege: A Theory of Social Stratification*. New York: McGraw-Hill.

Lenski, Gerhard E. 2005. *Ecological-Evolutionary Theory: Principles and Applications*. Boulder: Paradigm.

Lenski, Gerhard, and Jean Lenski. 1987. *Human Societies: An Introduction to Macrosociology*. 5th ed. New York: McGraw-Hill.

Lenski, Gerhard, Jean Lenski, and Patrick Nolan. 1991. *Human Societies: An Introduction to Macrosociology*. 7th ed. New York: McGraw-Hill.

Margolis, Maxine, and Conrad Kottak. 2003. "A Biographical Essay about Marvin Harris." *American Anthropologist* 105(3): 685–688.

Merton, Robert K. 1968. *Social Theory and Social Structure*. New York: Free Press.

Miller, Roger L. 2004. *Economics Today: The Macro View*. 12th ed. New York: Addison-Wesley.

Mills, C. Wright. 1951/1973. *White Collar: The American Middle Classes*. New York: Oxford University Press.

Mills, C. Wright. 1958. *The Causes of World War Three*. London: Secker and Warburg.

Mills, C. Wright. 1956/1970. *The Power Elite*. New York: Oxford University Press.

Mills, C. Wright. 1959/1976. *The Sociological Imagination*. New York: Oxford University Press.

Mills, C. Wright. 1963/1967. *Power, Politics, and People: The Collected Essays of C. Wright Mills*, edited by Irving L. Horowitz. New York: Oxford University Press.

Mills, C. Wright. 2000. *C. Wright Mills: Letters and Autobiographical Writings*, edited by K. Mills and P. Mills. Berkeley: University of California Press.

Monaghan, Charles. 1986, April. "Good to Eat: Riddles of Food and Culture" (book review). *Smithsonian* 17: 148–149.

Oakes, Guy, and Arthur Vidich. 1999. *Collaboration, Reputation, and Ethics in American Academic Life: Hans H. Gerth and C. Wright Mills.* Urbana: University of Illinois Press.

Parsons, Talcott. 1957, October. "The Distribution of Power in American Society." *World Politics* 10(1).

Phillips, Kevin. 2002. *Wealth and Democracy: A Political History of the American Rich.* New York: Broadway Books.

Sanderson, Stephen K. 1990. *Social Evolutionism: A Critical History.* Oxford, UK: Basil Blackwell.

Sanderson, Stephen K., 1999. *Social Transformations: A General Theory of Historical Development.* Lanham, MD: Rowman and Littlefield.

Sanderson, Stephen K., and Arthur Alderson. 2005. *World Societies: The Evolution of Human Social Life.* Boston: Pearson Education.

Summers, J. 2000, October. "The Big Discourse." *Nation* 271(10).

Wallerstein, Immanuel. 1974. *The Modern World-System: Capitalist Agriculture and the Origins of the European World-Economy in the Sixteenth Century.* New York: Academic Press.

Wallerstein, Immanuel. 1980. *The Modern World-System II: Mercantilism and the Consolidation of the European World-Economy, 1600–1750.* New York: Academic Press.

Wallerstein, Immanuel. 1989. *The Modern World-System III: The Second Era of Great Expansion of the Capitalist World-Economy, 1730–1840.* New York: Academic Press.

Wallerstein, Immanuel. 1998. *Utopistics; or, Historical Choices of the Twenty-first Century.* New York: W. W. Norton.

Wallerstein, Immanuel. 1999. *The End of the World as We Know It.* Minneapolis: University of Minnesota Press.

Wallerstein, Immanuel. 2000. *The Essential Wallerstein.* New York: The New Press.

Wallerstein, Immanuel. 2003. *The Decline of American Power.* New York: The New Press.

Index

abstracted empiricism, 25, 32
adaptations, 44, 108, 117, 120,
126–127; cumulative change
and, 108–109; elites and,
120; by individuals, 117,
120; infrastructural, 37
administration, 74, 124, 129, 130
administrators, 7
African American, 113
agrarian societies, 121, 123–124,
130; and elites, 135n, 142–
143; inequality and, 123–124,
130. *See also* agriculture
Agricultural Revolution, 49, 50–
53, 101n
agriculture, 4
alienation, 6, 18, 56–57, 96; and
rationalization, 21
American dream, 55
American Journal of Sociology, 31
America Now (Harris), 55, 70n.
See also Why Nothing Works
American Sociological Review, 31
Andrezejewski, Stanislaw, 123
anthropology, 38–39, 47, 76, 149.
See also social science
antimonopoly laws, 56. *See also*
monopoly; oligopoly
apathy, 14, 18–19
archaeology, 106
authority, 8, 9, 22; institutionalization of, 115–116; and retainer
class, 115–116. *See also* coercion; manipulation; power
automation, 6, 55, 56–57, 96
autonomy, 5, 6, 17–18, 56–57

baby boom, 64–65
beliefs, 4, 116, 122
Bierstedt, Robert, 34n

bifurcation, 79
Big Bazaar, 15. *See also* commodification
bio-psychological needs, 44–45.
See also human constants, selective principles
Black Death, 141–142
Braverman, Harry, 98, 148
bureaucracy, 1, 3, 4, 5, 55–56;
administration and, 129, 130;
agriculture and, 16–17;
alienation and, 16, 17–18, 21;
centralization and, 12, 13,
27–29, 57; characteristics of,
145; Chinese, 142; coordination of, 5, 28–29; core states
and, 82; cultural materialism
and, 55–56, 57, 72n; democracy and, 19–20; division of
labor and, 5–6; freedom and
reason and, 20–22, 27; human factors and, 9, 10, 16;
and elites, 3,4, 9–11; oligopoly and, 57; rationalization
and, 3, 16, 17, 21–22; rise of
capitalism and, 142; schools
and, 16, 150n; science and,
17; size of, 27–29; technology and, 16; uneven development of, 10; university
and, 23–24. *See also* bureaucratization; rationalization
bureaucratization, 7, 10, 11; capitalism and, 145–146; com-
plexity and, 146; decline of
social bond and, 148–149; intensification of production
and, 145–146, 149; organizational imperative and, 147–
148, 151n; population growth

eralism and, 85–86, 87–88, 125; limits of, 121; of management, 8; nationalism and, 79, 85, 112–113; social change and, 119–120; social sciences and, 27; socialist, 86. *See also* legitimation

idiographic scholarship, 75, 101n

immigration, 60, 62–63; economy and, 62, 63; fertility and, 62; geography and, 62–63; law and, 62–63; peripheral areas and, 93; politics and, 62–63; underclass and, 93. *See also* population

individualism, 148

inductive method, 103–104

industrialism, 10–14; capitalism and, 48–49, 53–54; inequality and, 123–124; as master trend, 138; world-systems and, 84. *See also* hyperindustrialism; industrial revolution

Industrial Revolution, 48, 49, 53–55; capitalism and, 53; intensification and, 53–54. *See also* industrialism

inequality, 105–106, 113–114; between societies, 126; division of labor and, 106; income, 125–126; intensification and, 122–126, 127–129; liberal reform and, 85–86; lower class and 129–130; power and, 113–114, 115; self-interest and, 105–106, 114; in the Soviet Union, 125–126; technology and, 121, 124–126; wealth and, 125, 128–129, 130

infanticide, 50

infrastructural determinism, 40, 43, 53, 69n; interpretations of, 120–121. *See also* fundamental innovations; infrastructure; primacy of infrastructure

infrastructure, 37, 38, 44; ecological-evolutionary theory and, 120; environment and, 48; of hyperindustrial society, 57–67; industrial revolution and, 54–55; primacy of, 37–38, 40, 43, 57–58; recent intensification of, 57–67; structure and, 48. *See also* infrastructural materialism; primacy of infrastructure

innovation, 117–120, 137–138; cultural information and, 118; diffusion and, 119; fundamental, 119; impediments to, 117, 143; ideologies and, 119; learning and, 107; physical environment and, 118–119; population size and, 118; rate of, 118–120; technology and, 120

Inquisition, 141

instinctual behavior, 14

institutions, 78

intellectual community, 3, 14, 22–23; apologists and, 23; default of, 22–23; moral insensibility and, 14; task of, 22. *See also* social sciences

intensification, 46–47; bureaucracy and, 66, 155; capitalism and, 53–54, 140–141; depletion and, 51–52, 54–55, 66; division of labor and, 67; dysfunctions of, 66; hunting and gathering and, 50–53; industrial revolution and, 53–55; inequality and, 122–126; population and, 52; rationalization and, 149. *See also* exponential growth infrastructure

interglacial period, 51–52

internal contradictions, 78–79; hegemony and, 81–88; Marx and, 89; world-system and, 88–90

See also cultural materialism; ecological-evolutionary theory
materialist, 1, 44
Mead, George Herbert, 2, 31
mental superstructure, 42. *See also* superstructure
mergers, 5
Merton, Robert K., 32
Mexico, 52–53
Michels, Robert, 106
Michigan, University of, 132, 133
Middle East, 52
middle range theory, 103
middle stratum, 12, 13, 115–116, 124, 129–130; and conflict, 13. *See also* management; white collar
migration, 60, 62–63; disorder and, 93. *See also* immigration, population
militarism, 1, 14, 28–29. *See also* military; power elite
military 10; cost of, 88; domination and, 74, 84–85; hegemony and, 87; limits, 121; service, 85, 123. *See also* elites
Military Industrial Complex, 23
Miller, Fred, 71n
Mills, C. Wright, 106, 115; communications technology and, 146–147; multicausality and, 138, 139–140; rise of capitalism and, 139–140
Moctezuma, 53
mode of production, 5, 37, 40, 41; economy and, 48; types of, 121–122, 135n. *See also* infrastructure
mode of reproduction, 37, 40–41. *See also* infrastructure
modernity, 74–75, 138–139
monopoly, 55–56, 81–82, 91, 151n
moral insensibility, 14, 17; and rationalization, 19
morality, 116

multicausality, 137–138, 145
Napoleon, 10
national interests, 35n
nationalism, 79, 85, 112–113
nation-state, 3–4, 73; capital accumulation and, 91–92, 123–124; as history making unit, 4; rivalry between, 86–87; sovereignty and, 83; weakening of power, 86, 88, 91–92; within world-system, 80–83
natural evolution, 106–108. *See also* evolution
Near East, 50
Netherlands, 87
Newcome, Thomas, 54
New Men of Labor (Mills), 99–100
New World, 50, 52–53, 144–145
1917, 85
1968, 85–86, 92, 100
1989, 92
Nolan, Patrick, 132–133
nomothetic science, 75
norms, 4, 116
North Carolina, University of, 132

occupational change, 4
Old World, 52
oligopoly, 55, 56, 57, 96, 151n; bureaucracy and, 57
organic evolution. *See* evolution; natural evolution
organization, 5
organizational imperative, 147–148
Origin of Species (Darwin), 107
outsourcing, 96

Pacific Rim, 96
paradigm, 38, 68, 106
Parsons, Talcott, 25, 31, 34n
peripheral states, 80, 81; economies and, 82; exploitation and, 84–85, 86; outsourcing and, 96; raw materials and, 84

permanent settlement, 52
persuasion, 15
Phillips, Kevin, 102n
physical environment, 37; constraints and, 40–41, 110–112, 119; inequality and, 123; infrastructure and, 37; population and, 119; social change and, 118–119. *See also* sociocultural environment
polarization, 82, 84, 86; capitalism and, 94; disorder and, 94; division of labor and, 82; migration and, 93; socialism and, 86
political economy, 41–42
political movements, 75
political science, 29, 103, 149
population, 37; age and sex structure of, 63–65; bureaucratization and, 146; checks on, 47, 60, 69n, 70n, 105, 110–111; cost/benefit and, 141–142; crisis of feudalism and, 140–141, 143; density and, 122; environment and, 105, 108, 111; exponential growth and, 49–50; fertility and, 60–62, 122; food production and, 38, 41, 44, 46–47, 105, 122; growth of, 47, 105; hunting and gathering societies and, 50; hyperindustrialism and, 59–61; inequality and, 125, 129–130; Malthus and, 38; migration and, 60, 62–63, 92, 122, 130; prestige and, 111; production and, 38, 47, 48, 105; rate of change and, 118; rise of capitalism and, 140–142; struggle for resources and, 110–111; technology and, 121–122. *See also* infrastructure; mode of reproduction

postindustrial society, 56–57. *See also* hyperindustrialism; service society
Powahatan, 53
power, 6, 8, 9, 11, 113; authority and, 8, 11; coercion and, 8; distribution of, 114, 122–126; groups and, 77–78; hegemonic, 87; manipulation and, 8–9; markets and, 80, 82; nation states and, 91–92; shift, 8–9; struggle for, 113–114. *See also* authority; manipulation
Power and Privilege (Lenski), 104, 109, 122, 123, 135n
The Power Elite (Mills), 2, 3, 7, 32, 34n
power elite, 10–11; common background of, 11; coordination among, 12, 28–29; democracy and, 20; liberal theory and, 12–13; middle levels and, 13; militarism of, 28–29
power shift, 8–9, 115–116
pragmatism, 2, 31
precapitalism, 9
predominant character, 4
preindustrial societies, 121
prestige, 6, 11, 111; consumption and, 111; struggle for, 113
primacy of the infrastructure, 37, 43, 49, 67; and ecological-evolutionary theory, 137. *See also* fundamental innovations; infrastructural determinism
primary groups, 147
pristine change, 119, 137
privatization, 58
productivity, 71n, 80, 111; self-interest and, 114, 124–125
professionalization, 6
professors, 23–24, 26
profit, 48, 53–54, 57, 79, 80; core industries and, 81–82, 96; decline of, 95–97, 130; squeeze

on, 92; by U.S. industry, 97–99. *See also* capital accumulation

progress, 85, 86; evolution and, 106–108; faith in, 86, 93

progressive forces, 94–95

race, 75, 78, 106, 113

radicalism, 85

rationality. *See* rationalization

rationalization, 3, 16, 67; agriculture and, 16–17; bureaucracy and, 149; capitalism and, 94; centralization and, 16; moral insensibility and, 19; reason and, 21–22; schools and, 16; science and, 3, 17; world-systems and, 90. *See also* bureaucracy; bureaucratization; formal rationality; intensification

reason, 3, 9, 17; democracy and, 27; rationalization and, 20, 21–22, 23

reciprocity, 74

reform. *See* liberal reform

Reformation, 141

relations of production, 47–48

religion, 9

resources, 105–106, 110–111; instability and, 111; struggle for, 111. *See also* depletion/pollution

retainer class. *See* mid-level; white collar

revolution, 115

The Rise of Anthropological Theory (Harris), 38, 67–68, 68n

role expectations, 7

routinization, 6

sacred, 116

salesmanship, 15–16; personality market and, 18. *See also* Big Bazaar; commodification; consumer culture; marketing

Sanderson, Stephen K., 39

Savery, Thomas, 54

secondary needs, 109–110, 111

selective principles, 44–45, 46. *See also* bio-psychological needs; human constants; human needs

self-interest, 105, 114

semiperiphery, 80, 81; economies and, 82; exploitation and, 84–85; function of, 84; outsourcing and, 96

service and information society, 4, 55, 56–57; growth of, 58–59, 97–98

service workers, 56, 98, 130

sex, 106

social bond, 148–149

social collapse, 20. *See also* extinction

social control, 112

social critic, 2

social disorder, 93–95

social evolution, 106–109; compared to organic, 106–108; cumulative change and, 108–109; energy, 46–47; hunting and gathering societies and, 50–51; population and, 46–47; in social science, 75. *See also* evolution

social institutions, 37, 39

socialism, 48, 86

socialization, 4, 11

social organization, 121. *See also* social structure

social psychology, 4

social science, 1, 2; bureaucracy and, 25–26, 76–77, 101n; classics and, 1, 2, 24–25, 37, 76–77, 103–104; deduction and induction in, 103–104; empiricism and, 24–25, 205; evolution in, 75; history and, 24, 75; ideology and, 27, 77–78; idiographic and, 75; level of analysis and, 73, 75, 76; micro-macro split and, 2, 76–

77, 103; natural sciences and,
23, 101n; nomothetic and, 75;
power and, 77–78; rationalization and, 3, 18; restructuring of, 75–77; role of, 22–26,
73, 150; as single discipline,
75–76; social justice and, 24–
25, 77–78, 79; sociological
imagination and, 26–27; specialization and, 23–24, 75–
77, 103; task of, 24, 68, 77–
78, 79; theory in, 24, 75; values and, 26, 77–78, 94–95.
See also intellectual community
Social Security, 64, 65
social stability, 43, 112–113, 116–
117, 134n; and centralization,
142
social structure, 2, 4, 27, 37; bureaucracy and, 138, 146–149;
capitalism and, 138; feedback
of, 37–38, 43–44, 46, 49; independent effects and, 48; integration of 12, 28–29; membership within, 77–78; population and, 122; world-system
and, 73. *See also* bureaucracy; capitalism; primary
group; social institution
social systems, 3–4, 37, 39, 55,
78–79; change and, 117; cumulative change and, 108–
109; hegemony and, 87–88;
as imperfect, 112–113; stability of, 38, 43, 116–117; tipping mechanism and, 82
social theory, 103, 104
sociocultural environment, 109,
112; change and, 119, 126–
127; contact and, 50–51, 127;
cultural materialism and,
137–138; ecological-
evolutionary theory and,
137–138; world-systems and,
126–127. *See also* cultural
contact

The Sociological Imagination
(Mills), 3, 32
sociological imagination 26–27
sociology, 29, 38–39, 75, 76, 103,
149
South East Asia, 50
Soviet Union, 124
Spencer, Herbert, 106, 107, 108
standardization, 116–117
status groups, 80
status inconsistency, 134n
stratification, 113–114; complexity of, 121; ecological theory
of, 122–126. *See also* inequality
structural perspective, 138, 145
subsistence technology, 121–122.
See also infrastructure; mode
of production
substantive rationality, 22, 94–95,
101n. *See also* formal rationality; rationalization
Summers, John, 36n
superstructure, 37, 42; feedback
and, 37–38, 43–44, 46, 49
surplus appropriation, 80, 115–
116, 125; inequality and,
122–126
survival need, 110

technicians, 115
technology, 4–5, 8, 37; communications and, 121, 146–147;
diffusion of, 144–145; inequality and, 122–126; innovation and, 117, 144–145;
population and, 121, 122;
power and, 16; transportation
and, 121. *See also* fundamental innovations; mode of production
Texas A&M University, 30, 31
*Theories of Culture in Post-
Modern Times* (Harris), 38,
69n
therapeutic power, 8, 9
tipping mechanism, 82

About the Author

Frank W. Elwell received a Ph.D. in sociology from the University at Albany and master's degrees from the University at Albany (sociology) and the State University of New York at New Paltz (political science/education). He began his teaching career at Murray State University in Kentucky, where he worked his way through the ranks to full professor, and then became the founding dean of liberal arts at Rogers State University in Oklahoma. Previous works include *Industrializing America* (Praeger), *A Commentary on Malthus's 1798 Essay as Social Theory* (Mellen), and *The Classical Tradition: Malthus, Marx, Weber, and Durkheim* (Internet). His areas of academic interest include social evolution, cultural ecology, and macrosocial theory. He is currently working on a manuscript covering additional contemporary social theorists as well as a book on evolutionary sociology.